What people are saying about

The God Who Sees You

"In *The God Who Sees You*, Tammy Maltby writes with her signature grace and compassion to point us toward the One who sees. I hope you will take your time with each chapter so these truths about God's love find their way into the deep places of your soul. It is a joy to rest in the promise of this book. *I am seen by God.* May those words keep taking your breath away."

Angela Thomas, best-selling author and speaker

"Are you living a 'this isn't the life I signed up for' life? Tammy Maltby understands that and offers much-needed hope. God sees you, loves you, and is actively involved in your life right now, even if you're going through a hard season. If you need hope and help, you'll find it in the pages of this book from a girlfriend who understands."

Jill Savage, author of *Real Moms ... Real Jesus*
and founder and CEO of Hearts at Home

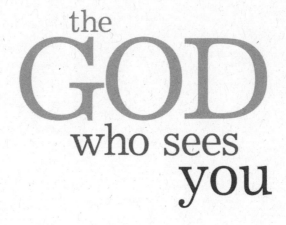

the
GOD
who sees
you

Also by Tammy Maltby

LifeGiving: Discovering the Secrets to a Beautiful Life

with Tamra Farah

LifeGiving: A Discovery Journal to a Beautiful Life

with Tamra Farah

Confessions of a Good Christian Girl

with Anne Christian Buchanan

Confessions of a Good Christian Guy

with Tom Davis

The Christmas Kitchen: A Gathering Place for Making Memories

with Anne Christian Buchanan

Revitalize Your Spiritual Life

contributor

the
GOD
who sees
you

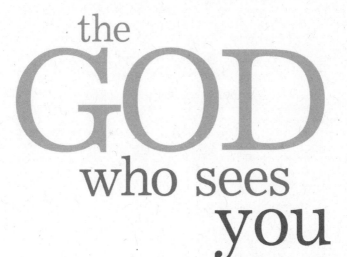

*Look to Him When You
Feel Discouraged, Forgotten,
or Invisible*

Tammy Maltby
with Anne Christian Buchanan

David C Cook®
transforming lives together

THE GOD WHO SEES YOU
Published by David C Cook
4050 Lee Vance View
Colorado Springs, CO 80918 U.S.A.

David C Cook Distribution Canada
55 Woodslee Avenue, Paris, Ontario, Canada N3L 3E5

David C Cook U.K., Kingsway Communications
Eastbourne, East Sussex BN23 6NT, England

David C Cook and the graphic circle C logo are registered
trademarks of Cook Communications Ministries.

All rights reserved. Except for brief excerpts for review purposes, no part of this book
may be reproduced or used in any form without written permission from the publisher.

The website addresses recommended throughout this book are offered as a
resource to you. These websites are not intended in any way to be or imply an
endorsement on the part of David C Cook, nor do we vouch for their content.

For reasons of privacy, names and pertinent details of some of the people
profiled in this book have been changed. However, each story is absolutely
true. Permission has been granted for personal stories used throughout.

Unless otherwise noted, Scripture quotations are taken from the *Holy Bible, New
International Version*®. *NIV*®. Copyright © 1973, 1978, 1984 by International Bible
Society. Used by permission of Zondervan. All rights reserved. Scripture quotations
marked MSG are taken from *THE MESSAGE*. Copyright © by Eugene H. Peterson
1993, 1994, 1995, 1996, 2000, 2001, 2002. Used by permission of NavPress Publishing
Group; NLT are taken from the New Living Translation of the Holy Bible. New Living
Translation copyright © 1996, 2004, 2007 by Tyndale Charitable Trust. Used by
permission of Tyndale House Publisher. (Quotation of Mark 6:22–24 in chapter 7 is
from the 1996 version of the NLT.); NKJV are taken from the New King James Version.
Copyright © 1982 by Thomas Nelson, Inc. Used by permission. All rights reserved; KJV
are from the King James Version of the Bible. (Public Domain.); NASB are taken from the
New American Standard Bible, © Copyright 1960, 1995 by The Lockman Foundation.
Used by permission; NRSV are taken from the New Revised Standard Version Bible,
copyright 1989, Division of Christian Education of the National Council of the Churches
of Christ in the United States of America. Used by permission. All rights reserved.

The author has added italics to Scripture quotations for emphasis.

LCCN 2012930870
ISBN 978-1-4347-6799-8
eISBN 978-0-7814-0845-5

© 2012 Tammy Maltby

Published in association with the William K. Jensen Literary
Agency, 119 Bampton Court, Eugene, Oregon 97404.

The Team: Susan Tjaden, Nick Lee, Caitlyn York, Karen Athen.
Cover Design: Amy Konyndyk
Cover Image: iStockPhoto

Printed in the United States of America

First Edition 2012

1 2 3 4 5 6 7 8 9 10

012911

To my first two grandchildren, Cohen Michael
Tamayo and Noble Nikolai Scroggins.
May this be your legacy from me:
to know the God who sees you.

contents

acknowledgments

It is through the lives and actions of many that I have seen the faithfulness of the God who sees me. With great appreciation and affection, I would like to offer my gratitude:

To my cocreator, Anne Christian Buchanan. The very reality of this book is a story of how God saw us. Thank you for your hard work and profound dedication to this book. You are a gift.

To the excellent people at David C Cook. Thank you for believing in this important message.

To my literary agent, Bill Jensen, my longtime friend, a lover of all things beautiful. Thank you for your encouragement.

To the dear friends who have loved me in the most difficult times of my life and have celebrated its restoration, especially my sisters, Twyla Beyers and Terri Johnson; my brother, Dean Hanson; and longtime friends Paul and Maryjo Valder, Steve and Lynn Brown, Tom and Emily Davis, Gary and Lisa Black, Tom and Tracy Hoogenboom.

My amazing, godly parents, Kenneth and Ramona Hanson—married sixty-two faithful years. What a legacy you have left your family. What a privilege to be your youngest daughter. I love you dearly.

To my beloved children, Mackenzie Maltby Tamayo, Tatiana Maltby Scroggins, Samuel Maltby, and Mikia Maltby, plus my wonderful sons-in-love Zac Tamayo and Ben Scroggins. You are the inspiration in everything I do and every choice I make. Words are simply weak in expressing the profound love I have for you and the joy I have in you. Being your mother has been the greatest gift I have ever received. You are His arrows entering a generation I never will, taking His message of mercy, grace, and forgiveness to places I could only dream of. I hope you'll continue to live with great passion and choose joy always. He sees you.

To the Bear, who has taught me that love is the best part of any story. Thank you for dancing with me beyond the fire.

And to the God who sees me: I rest in You alone.

Tammy Maltby

chapter one

please see me!

She gave this name to the LORD who spoke to her:
"You are the God who sees me,"
for she said, "I have now seen the One who sees me."

Genesis 16:13

It was late afternoon.

I sat on a bench in Washington's National Airport, leaning up against some kind of glass wall, my heavy winter coat, overpacked carry-on, magazine, and water bottle in a pile around me.

And I was crying.

That's just not like me. I don't cry easily, and certainly not in airports.

So why was I sitting there in tears? Partly because I was exhausted from a long speaking trip and still had several more days to go. Partly because I had missed my flight and would have to wait four hours for another one. Partly because I was homesick.

But mostly because everything I cared about in my life seemed to be falling apart.

After years of struggle, my twenty-year marriage had ended. Not surprisingly, my four teenagers were having a hard time—acting out in school, erupting in anger, withdrawing sullenly. And though I tried hard, I knew I wasn't always there for them. I had been too depressed and anxious that year even to put up a Christmas tree. I was struggling financially, and losing our home was a real possibility. And on top of it all, I had recently learned that my beloved, responsible—and unwed— firstborn, Mackenzie, was pregnant at age nineteen.

I had never felt more desperately alone.

As I sat there, watching the other travelers rush by me, I felt something else.

Invisible.

No one noticed my tears. No one stopped to ask if I was all right. No one knew the profound disappointment I was living with—the heartache, the loneliness, the pain that engulfed me like a tsunami.

It was just too much—more than I thought I could bear. Even though I've been a Christian almost all my life, even though God had proved Himself faithful to me again and again, I still felt myself whispering, "God, are You there? Are You paying attention?"

At that painful moment, it seemed no one saw me. That no one cared. That no one could help. Not even God.

feeling unseen

Have you ever felt that way? Do you feel that way now?

Mother Teresa is widely quoted as saying, "There is more hunger for love and appreciation in this world than for bread."[1] I believe that's true because I've been there and because I've met so many others who have been there too—people who are starving to be recognized and acknowledged, appreciated and affirmed, loved and cared for. Every day, it seems, I meet people who struggle with the sense that no one notices them, no one cares:

- moms who work insane hours—earning a living, cooking, cleaning, caring for children—and feel no one appreciates what they do.
- husbands and fathers who are convinced they are little more than "just a paycheck" to their families.
- employees who feel like nameless cogs in a machine.
- children who assume no one really cares who they are and what they want to say.
- teenagers convinced that no one understands them or cares what they think.
- young adults who can't figure out where they fit into the world.
- "geeky" girls and "nerdy" boys who are noticed only by their tormentors.
- gorgeous young men and women who feel like nothing more than a pretty face or an "abs of steel" body.
- single parents who struggle hard without ever quite making it.

- successful people who think they'd be nobody if they ever lost their jobs.
- addicts who feel they must conceal their habits at any cost.
- seniors who are sure they've joined the ranks of the invisible.
- sick people who are tired of being "just a disease" to their health-care workers.
- homeless people who watch people walk past them on the street.
- the poor and the unemployed who become "issues" instead of persons.
- pastors and people in ministry who don't dare let anyone in on their personal struggles.
- Christians whose efforts to obey God seem unappreciated and unsuccessful.
- ordinary men and women whose daily efforts seem to get them nowhere.

Any of these descriptions sound familiar? All these are people who need to know, really *know*, that they are seen. They need the message first voiced in the Bible by a woman named Hagar.

a slave's story

You can find Hagar's story in the book of Genesis, chapter 16. It's the story of an Egyptian slave girl who is used and abused and eventually runs away. It's also the story of the only woman in the Bible to give God a new name. Most important, it's the story of a woman whose life is transformed when she finally realizes she's really not invisible—that there is a God who sees her and cares about her plight and provides for her even at the lowest moment of her life.

We first meet Hagar when she's laboring as a maidservant in the camp of Abram and Sarai. She's essentially a nobody in that household. No one pays her any attention unless they want something—a pot scrubbed, a basket carried, an errand run. Or her body for sex, because even that area of her life is under someone else's control. Sarai, who is childless, compels Hagar to sleep with Abram in the hopes that the maid will produce a son for Sarai to raise. But when Hagar obeys and does become pregnant, Sarai turns jealous and abusive.

Hagar isn't entirely blameless, though. She flaunts her pregnancy, knowing that Sarai's barrenness is a sore subject. Then, when Sarai overreacts, Hagar decides to run away. The only place she can run is the desert, a very dangerous place for a pregnant girl with no food or water and no idea where she's going.

Finally, when her swollen feet can carry her no farther, Hagar slumps down beside a roadside well. I imagine her leaning against a rock, exhausted and ravenous as only a pregnant woman can be. Alone, afraid, probably still angry—and with no clue what to do next.

That's when the angel appears, bringing Hagar a message from a God she barely knows. The angel doesn't say that Hagar's life will get easier. He doesn't help her find food or another place to live. In fact, he tells her to return to Abram and Sarai, have her baby, and name him Ishmael. By the way, this Ishmael will grow up to be a hostile, combative "wild donkey of a man."[2] Not the most promising prophecy ever made! But Hagar is thrilled with it—not because of what it says, but because of what it *means*.

After all, this God who sent her a message actually knows her name. The angel addresses her as "Hagar, servant of Sarai."[3]

Even better, this God is aware of her predicament. The angel says it clearly: "The LORD has heard of your misery."[4]

Now let that sink in. God has heard Hagar cry out. He sees the reality of her life. Amazingly, this God has a future in mind for her and her son. In fact, her descendants through Ishmael will be too many to number.

Once Hagar realizes all this, she can't hold back her enthusiasm over what has happened to her. She even gives this foreign God a new name, one that will still be remembered centuries later.

She calls him El Roi, which literally means "the God who sees."

She blurts out, her voice thick with wonder, "I have now seen the One who sees me."[5]

ookamee!

I never fully understood the power of Hagar's affirmation until I began to share its message with others. I've been deliberately doing that for several years now, both in my professional speaking and my personal encounters. Each time I do, I'm stunned by the impact this seemingly simple message has on others.

It seems like I can teach and talk and write all day, I can attempt to lay all sorts of wisdom and practical insight on people—but the minute I whisper, "God *sees* you," something amazing happens. Rooms grow quiet. People begin to weep. It's as if there's a tender nerve in almost everyone when it comes to this loving and most aware God.

I think it's because so many of us—like Hagar, like me—often feel forgotten, ignored, discouraged, and invisible. All of us, deep down inside, have a heart-deep longing to be seen—really seen. This desire to be noticed, recognized, acknowledged—*known*—just seems to be intertwined with our DNA. It's foundational to who we are as human beings.

My grandson Cohen certainly has it. When he comes over to my house, he gets my attention moment to moment with his cries of "Look at me! Look at me!" Only he says it as one word: *Ookamee!*

When he's climbing on a jungle gym, when he thinks up a new trick, when he's mastered a new skill, I hear that gleeful little voice: "Ookamee! Ookamee!" I heard that same cry from my own four children when they were little.

But Cohen doesn't just want to be looked at. He wants his little-boy accomplishments to be acknowledged and affirmed and applauded. He wants to feel important and loved. He wants to know that I care and I'm close enough to help him if he needs it. That I'm right there with him, every step of the way—watching, caring, praising, affirming, and yes, smiling. He wants to know that in my eyes, he's the biggest, most amazing guy around.

And that's exactly what he gets, because I'm crazy about my grandson. Just by being himself, he makes me smile. And Cohen *knows* he's the apple of my eye. He's absolutely confident that I delight in him and won't let anything bad happen to him.

Don't you wish we all had that kind of confidence in God?

I believe that in every one of us, deep in our spirits, is a child crying, "Ookamee!" We long to know that our heavenly Father sees us, and we need other people to see us as well. As with Cohen, this longing is for more than just simple attention. Our heart-deep yearning to be seen involves so much more. We long to be:

- *affirmed* as worthwhile, as deserving a place on this earth.
- *valued* for what makes us unique and special—not just how we look or what we do, but who we are inside.
- *appreciated* not only for our accomplishments, but also for our intentions and our efforts.
- *assured* that we make a difference—to hear "well done" from someone who really understands what we are doing!
- *connected* through social bonds, family ties, and intimate relationships—accepted as an indispensable part of a group.
- *desired* and *celebrated* by someone who enjoys us and wants to be with us.
- *cared for* by someone who perceives our needs and is willing and able to help meet them.
- *included* in someone's plans, confident that someone takes our long-term best interests to heart and can help us find a purpose for the future.

Above all, of course, we long to be *loved.* This is the heart of all these other needs. We have a deep desire to be seen by someone who loves us no matter what—past, present, and future. Someone who is committed to us and can love us with unconditional love, even when we're less than lovable—even, in fact, when we are at our most unlovable.

a hitch in the plan

There's a reason we all have those yearnings. It's because God made us that way. It's part of God's original design for us. We were made to live openly with Him and one another in the clean, clear light of Eden. Seeing and being seen without shame. Loving and being loved without fear. Caring and being cared for without mixed motives. Knowing one another. Naming one another. Enjoying one another in innocent intimacy and simple trust and endless fellowship with the God who saw us in His mind's eye before He ever shaped us out of clay.

From the beginning, "ookamee" and "I love you" were designed to go hand in hand.

But you know what happened to that original vision, don't you? Sin happened. Disobedience dawned. And then this whole business of seeing and being seen got complicated.

According to the Bible, the first humans made a deliberate choice to go against God, and that choice forever changed the way they looked at God and each other. Once they sinned—or even considered the possibility—they began looking at their Creator with distrust: "Why didn't He want us to eat that fruit? What is He withholding from me? What's He going to do now?"

Suddenly, being seen didn't seem like such a wonderful proposition.

They looked down in shame at their naked, vulnerable bodies and thought, "I can't let anyone see who I am. I've got to cover up."

They also looked at each other with resentment and fear: "I've got to be careful. I can't let down my guard with you. What if you betray me? What if who I am isn't enough for you?"

Suddenly there they were, crouching behind the bushes, still yearning to be seen because that need was part of who they were, yet absolutely terrified that the truth of who they were and what they'd done would be revealed. They avoided each other's glances and tried their best to escape the notice of the One they needed most of all.

Once sin and brokenness arrived on this planet, "ookamee" became hide–and–seek—with an emphasis on "hide."

the hide-and-seek dilemma

Sadly, we've been living that hide-and-seek reality ever since. Yet we are reluctant to experience the reality we so long for.

We're still Adam and Even hiding in the garden, crouching behind a bush. We've gotten a glimpse of ourselves—naked, unappealing, vulnerable—and we don't like what we see. We can't imagine that anyone can see us as we are and still love us.

So we hide.

We all do it—every single one of us. Most of us, as we go through life, grow adept at hiding parts of our life from other people and from ourselves. Even though we may realize in our heads that God sees us, we still attempt to hide from Him.

We hide for the same reasons the first humans did. Because of sin. Our own sin, which makes us guilty and ashamed. The sin of others, which hurts us and teaches us to fear and distrust, as well as tempting us to sin some more. And the sinful condition of this fallen world, which makes it hard to even imagine living any other way.

We hide because we have been wounded in the past. Like Hagar, we've been used and abused—laughed at, admonished, betrayed, abandoned, taken advantage of—or simply ignored, treated as less than beloved children of God. We hide because we are terrified to let any of that happen again. We also hide because we're ashamed of our shortcomings and inadequacies. We've failed and messed up and don't want to be punished or found out. We're convinced that we're ugly and unworthy, that no one could love us if they really saw us. We hide because we feel confused or afraid or guilty—or just because hiding has become a habit. We've hidden so long that we don't have a clue how to reveal ourselves to God or anyone else.

And let's admit it: Often we hide because we want our own way. I know this is true of me at times. Sometimes I just don't want the light of truth to penetrate my choices. There's a certain power in not being seen. Staying hidden and secret can be a way of hanging on to control, choosing what to let others see and what to keep to ourselves.

Of course, all this is a delusion when it comes to God—because God can see us anyway and because the truth is, we're not in control at all. Still, all too often, we hold on to our habits of hiding, fooling ourselves into believing we can put something over on God.

We hide by stretching the truth … or by lying outright. We hide by guarding secrets and by presenting ourselves selectively. We deflect the truth by steering conversation away from areas we don't want to visit. We duck phone calls and ignore emails and stay away from the mailbox. We avoid bringing up certain topics to avoid conflict.

Some of us grow adept at hiding in plain sight. We make a point of being open and honest and easy to know—except when it comes to certain vulnerable parts of our lives. We may even learn to hide our hearts by sharing our bodies, using outer nakedness to cover up inward pain.

Does any of this sound familiar? I'm sorry to say, it does to me. All too often, hide-and-seek is simply the way we live.

Don't get me wrong—hiding isn't always a bad strategy when it comes to other people. There are times when we do need to conceal parts of our lives and protect our hearts. The truth is, with sin a reality, the world isn't a safe place, and we just can't run around naked anymore. Even Jesus controlled the way He revealed Himself in the world.

But here's why hiding becomes a problem: It's hard to hide without being lonely. It's hard to hide from God's light without getting swallowed in darkness. The more we hide, the more our inborn need to be seen is thwarted, and the more we feel no one hears us or sees us or cares about us.

Whether it's because we're personally in hiding or because we're all caught up in a world that lives by smoke and mirrors, the results are the same.

Hide-and-seek … and hunger.

People yearning to be seen … and feeling invisible.

People who have a hard time seeing the God who sees them.

do we believe God sees us?

A lot of these hurting people are Christians. They're people who know Jesus, who read the Bible, who believe in miracles. And still, somehow, they have trouble getting it through their heads and hearts that God really does see them. They "know" God sees everything. They "know" God loves them and cares for them. But where is the happy confidence, the bedrock awareness that God is right there, affirming and applauding and guiding every step?

The longer I live in this world and the more I talk to women and men across the United States, the more I've come to believe that many of us have never fully taken to heart this reality about God. And our hearts are heavy as a result. We were created to be confident, loving, secure children who rejoice that God has a job for us and can use us for the benefit of His kingdom. Instead, too much of the time, even God's people live like lonely, hurting children, whispering, "Please see me," in a world where we feel forgotten and overlooked.

the story of our lives

Not long ago, I accompanied a friend to the hospital for surgery. After she was wheeled away, I began talking with one of the nurses. Somehow the conversation came around to the nurse's brother, who had been killed in an accident three years earlier. Like most untimely losses, the brother's death had dramatically disrupted this woman's family. Her mother still struggled with bitterness. Her parents' marriage had faltered. Her son, born two weeks after her brother's death, would never know his uncle.

Soon my new friend was pouring out her heart to me. And at some point I shared with her what I was learning about El Roi.

"Do you understand that God sees you in all this?" I said. "He really *sees*—"

I hadn't even finished the sentence before she started to weep. She cried so hard that another nurse walked over to see if she was okay. She was completely undone at the thought that God saw her pain, her fear, her broken heart. She kept saying through deep sobs, "He sees me? He really sees me?"

That was just one simple encounter, one more reminder that the message of the God who sees you is one that needs to be shared again and again—with those who don't know the Lord and with those who do. Remember, there's a reason we hunger to be recognized, acknowledged, appreciated, and cared for. There's a reason our hide-and-seek lives leave us feeling so bruised and unsatisfied. It's because God has intentionally and wonderfully created us to see and be seen, to live in intimate and joyful relationship with Him and with others.

More important, He put that need in us *because He wants to meet it*. He's put the longing there to draw us closer to His heart.

We hunger to be seen—because He really does see us.

The challenge is to really believe it … to live in the confidence that we are recognized and accepted and included and, most of all, loved.

Can you do that? Can I?

I'll admit I've had my struggles, but I can honestly say I believe it with all my heart. Here's why.

First, the Bible tells me so, and the Bible has proven a reliable guide in my life. The whole sweep of the Bible can be understood as the story of a God who saw His people, even when they couldn't see Him. A God who came to earth and paid special attention to the unnoticed—the meek and the mourning, the children everyone turned away, the powerless rather than the ones on top. A God who cared so much about what He saw that He came to earth in human form, turning hide-and-seek into the ultimate show-and-tell.

But I also believe because God has shown me, again and again, in the circumstances of my life. He has shown me through the whisper of His Holy Spirit, through the timing of my experiences, through the love and example of other people and the mysterious provision of what I have needed most.

I've seen too much evidence *not* to believe God sees me. I've been loved too much not to make it the story of my life.

I want it to be the story of your life as well. I want it to change everything, including the way you look at God and yourself and other people. I want you to live in confidence that when God looks at you, He sees beauty. He sees value. He sees hope. And that even when you're hiding, or when you're so beaten down you can't see anything clearly, He's still hard at work, crafting a beautiful future of relationship with Him and with others.

the reality that changes everything

When Hagar really got her heart around the amazing reality that God saw her, everything changed.

Well, not everything. Hagar still had to go back into slavery. She still had to deal with her life circumstances and choices.

So what changed? Hagar did. Her entire outlook shifted. She started looking at her life differently, and eventually that did change everything. Hagar returned to her old life with a new confidence, a new attitude toward the future. She held tightly to the angel's promise. Though she sometimes faltered, she kept moving forward. The last time we see her in Genesis, she's busy trying to find a wife for her grown son.

I've experienced that kind of shift in my life since that airport moment. Because I, too, had an encounter that day with the God who sees me. It wasn't anything as dramatic as an angel at a well. But it was powerful enough to turn my head around and move me in a new and healing direction.

I felt it as I sat there weeping on the bench, leaning against the glass wall, with my belongings piled around me—a clear but gentle nudge from the Holy Spirit: *Turn around.*

Turn around?

Instantly, the theological implications swarmed through my head. *Is God telling me He has a new direction for my life? Does He want me to repent or change the way I'm living?*

No, no, insisted the quiet voice in my spirit, the one I've come to recognize as the Lord's. *I mean literally turn around.*

In my seat? That seemed strange. But I swiveled to look at the glass wall behind me, the one I'd been leaning against. It turned out to be the front window of a bookstore. And there, front and center, sat a book by Angela Thomas: *My Single Mom Life.*[6]

I know Angela. I even knew she was writing that book, though I hadn't seen it yet. I certainly never expected it to appear right before my eyes as a response to the Lord's prompting. Yet I knew in my spirit that its presence was a message for me.

I walked into the bookstore and bought the book. Over the next four hours—the rest of my unexpected layover—I read the whole thing. And God ministered to me powerfully in that time. He showed me I wasn't alone. He reminded me of the perils of self-pity but also of His sustaining power for my life. He assured me, once again: *I see you. I see your needs and your family's needs—even the painful realities you are afraid to let anyone know. I am able to protect you and provide for you, and I want to do it. You just need to turn around and see what I have to give you.*

That's the message I want to pass along to you from the start—my personal witness as someone who at times has felt forgotten, uncared for, unloved, invisible. I truly believe I have a word from God for those lonely, aching times in your life.

The message is this: Regardless of how you may *feel,* God does see you.

He knows your name, and He loves you—passionately and tenderly.

He sees your needs, and He yearns to fill them.

At any given moment, even when you feel most alone, He is working out a plan for your future.

All you have to do is turn around. Trust Him. Wait for Him. Keep your eyes open.

One way or another, one day soon, you will realize that you, too, have encountered El Roi.

And you, too, will be able to say, thankfully, "I have seen the God who sees me."

chapter two

the God who sees

Blessed be the name of God, forever and ever....
He opens up the depths, tells secrets, sees in
the dark—light spills out of him!
God of all my ancestors, all thanks! all praise!...
You've shown us what we asked for.

Daniel 2:20, 22–23 MSG

It was a typical Minnesota December day, which means the snow was deep, the temperature was near zero, and the sun was shining. I had flown in from Colorado to visit my mom and dad. We gathered at the little round table in their kitchen to enjoy our coffee and cookies—a typical Scandinavian after-breakfast treat—while gazing out the big kitchen windows at the sparkling landscape.

Suddenly, right in front of our window, there was an eruption of red. About twenty brilliantly colored cardinals descended on my parents' lawn. I had never seen that many of them in one place. But the sight of them was breathtaking—all that scarlet against the glistening white snow. It was like a Christmas card—or an impromptu pageant staged just for us.

We all smiled at one another across the table. "Can you believe this?" I said. "God's really showing off for us today!"

Then someone said, "He's giving us a gift, a little token to show He sees us and is thinking of us. That's just the way He is."

And it's true. Once again, in a quietly spectacular way, we'd been given a glimpse of the God who sees us, the opportunity to learn a little more about who He is and what He's like.

This is the God who, if He chooses, arranges wonderful little shows for our benefit, just to remind us that He cares, that He hasn't forgotten us. In so many ways, day in and day out, in little ways and large, He reaches out to us, reminding us that we're never invisible to Him.

But do we see Him? Do we trust His words and appreciate His ways? Have we truly taken to heart who He is? The better we get to know God, the easier it is to believe that He really does see us and that it's a good thing He does.

He's not *just* the God who sees us, of course. He has many other facets to His personality. That's why He's called by so many names in the Bible—not just El Roi, but Elohim ("Strong One"), El Shaddai ("All-Sufficient One"), El Olam ("Everlasting God"), and many others. We see Him in different persons or roles—Father, Son, and Holy Spirit—and get to know Him through many descriptions—Shepherd, Rock, King, Counselor, jealous Lover, living Word, Light of the world, Bridegroom, even Mother Hen.[1]

God is so big, so wonderful, so complex, it's impossible to capture Him with a single description. But that doesn't mean we can't know Him. For El Roi has been showing Himself to His children from the very moment of creation, when He first turned on the lights.

the God who sees you … is a God of light

Have you ever taken a cavern tour, where you followed a guide deep into the earth to view the rock formations? You walk on little lit paths, admiring the stalagmites and stalactites. Then, at some point, the guide will turn out the lights, and you literally can't see a thing. Deep in the earth, where the sun's light cannot penetrate, you really begin to appreciate how much you need the light.

Life-giving energy, truth-revealing brightness, the essence of warmth and freedom—that's light. It makes all vision possible, because our eyes don't work in the dark. It makes *life* possible because it fuels growth. Physically and spiritually, it combats fear and deception and pushes back evil.

According to the Bible, light is not just God's first creation. It's His very essence. The apostle John declares it: "God *is* light; in him there is no darkness at all."[2]

That's the first thing we need to know about the God who sees us: He's light, the source of all vision and freedom and growth. He's the One who viewed a newly illuminated planet and declared it good. He created a man and a woman in His own image—that is, made for the light—and declared that work to be *very* good. He called the first humans out of the dark shadows when they disobeyed Him and then hid themselves. And finally, He had to evict them from their sunlit garden home because the light of His truth and purity could not coexist with the darkness of their sin and disobedience.

Even then, God continued to provide light so His people could see. He came to them in the wilderness as a pillar of fire, lighting their nighttime travel.[3] He revealed Himself to the psalmist as a lamp for the feet and a light for the path.[4] Through the prophets, He promised light when His people were stumbling in darkness.[5]

Then, of course, God sent Jesus, who proclaimed, "I am the light of the world. Whoever follows me will never walk in darkness."[6] And He called us to shine as well—to reflect His light in a dark world so that others can see Him and know Him.[7]

The God who sees us is a God of light who makes it possible for us to see. He is truth and wisdom, enabling us to find our way even in the dark. But when it comes to actually seeing this God of light, things get a little more complicated.

the God who sees you …
is an unseen God

When my friend Lorraine's daughter was small, she loved to play hide-and-seek, but she couldn't quite grasp the main concept. When it was her turn to hide, she would just stand in the middle of the room and cover her eyes. She couldn't see anybody else, so she just assumed nobody could see her either.

I think it's easy to fall back on that kind of thinking when it comes to God. When we can't see Him, we start wondering if maybe He can't see us either. And the truth is, most of the time, we *can't* see Him.

John the Baptist stated up front that "no one has ever seen God, not so much as a glimpse."[8] Jesus spoke to a crowd about "your Father, who is unseen."[9] Both the apostle Paul and the author of Hebrews spoke of an "invisible" God.[10] Paul even insisted that "we fix our eyes not on what is seen, but on what is unseen"—namely, the eternal God.[11]

God is physically invisible to us because He is spirit, not matter. Our retinas and optic nerves were never intended to discern the One who created them.

God does sometimes reveal Himself through something we perceive visually—a burning bush or a pillar of cloud or an angel or, most important, a human being named Jesus. But even in the Bible (and in this book), when we speak of "seeing" God, we're almost always talking metaphorically.

To see God means to perceive Him, to be aware of His presence, to open our spiritual eyes to His reality—not to actually experience Him through our physical eyes. And even such spiritual seeing is not a constant in our human experience. No one sees God all the time, even with the eyes of the spirit.

But the fact that we can't physically see God isn't the real issue, is it? The real difficulty is that the unseen God is also hard to understand. His actions often don't make sense to us, and He doesn't look at things at all the way we do. Isaiah puts it this way:

"For my thoughts are not your thoughts,
    neither are your ways my ways,"
        declares the LORD.
"As the heavens are higher than the earth,
    so are my ways higher than your ways
    and my thoughts than your thoughts."[12]

To our limited understanding, God's ways are mysterious and often counterintuitive. There are even times when, for reasons we can't fathom, God hides Himself completely from us.[13] When that happens, it's so easy for us to get wrong ideas about Him. We get all mixed up about what we can see and what we can't see. And that's when we may fall into the trap of wanting to tell God what to do.

Have you ever tried to do that? It's one of my primary pitfalls. I tend to think I see and understand a lot more than I do. I jump to conclusions about what needs to happen in my life, what would make my children happy, what God should be doing and should not be doing. My prayers too easily morph into executive orders. My expectations emerge from my personal opinions. I'm afraid I just love to give God a good idea!

But the reality is, as long as I am living here on earth, both my physical and my spiritual vision are severely limited. No matter how clearly I think I see, all I really get is a blurry image of reality. Paul famously called it "a poor reflection as in a mirror."[14] Or as *The Message* puts it, I'm "squinting in a fog, peering through a mist."

As a result, I almost never see what the unseen, mysterious God sees so vividly.

The big picture.

the God who sees you … sees everything

To say that God sees what we don't is of course the biggest understatement of all time. God's vision encompasses everything that is, everything that has been, and everything that is yet to come. I love the picture that Psalm 33 paints:

> From heaven the LORD looks down
> and sees all mankind;
> from his dwelling place he watches
> all who live on earth—
> he who forms the hearts of all,
> who considers everything they do.[15]

God sees the entire sweep of history, from the dawn of creation to the end of time—for He Himself is the beginning and the end, the Alpha and the Omega. He sees the way one event leads into another, the way small things lead to big things.

He sees our world from a distance—the big picture that includes galaxies and stars and black holes and cosmic dust and our tiny, shimmering green and gold and blue planet where He has invested so much of Himself. But He sees it from incredibly close in as well. He notices each individual sparrow, each little blade of grass.[16]

More important, God notices each one of us, individually—each breath we take, each individual hair on our heads. He keeps track of the neurons and synapses that shape our thoughts and impressions, the hormones that inform our emotions. He sees our secrets, the inner realities nobody else sees, and the hidden spiritual world that is invisible to our eyes. He understands how our decisions and actions influence the unfolding of events and how these events in turn influence us.

And somehow, in a way that is eternally beyond me, God manages to hold this whole big picture together, to see it all at once. He observes the incredibly detailed tapestry of cause and effect, the flow of events through history—weather and earthquakes and gravity and cultures and political upheaval, human beings interacting with one another and the natural world, ideas intersecting with events.

All these things that boggle our minds pose no problem for the God who made it all. He sees it—all of it. And none of it fazes Him, even the dark things that have infected the universe for so long, because He knows how it all turns out. He is, in the words of an ancient prayer, "Almighty God, unto whom all hearts are open, all desires known, and from whom no secrets are hid."[17] It's all there, laid out before Him at any moment.

Which, to be honest, isn't necessarily comforting … unless you add one important reality.

Love.

the God who sees you … loves you

I can't think of anything more frightening than to be seen, really seen, by someone who doesn't truly love me.

Can you?

To be vulnerable to someone who doesn't have my best interests at heart. To be laid bare to the judgment of someone who sees me accurately and in detail but has no concern for my welfare. Or to be observed from a distance, like a bacteria on a microscope slide, by someone who has no intention of getting involved. That would be awful.

Yet I've talked to many people who think God looks at us like that. Or they see Him as Santa Claus in that scary old children's song that warns, "You better watch out!"—because He's keeping an eye on you, watching you while you're sleeping or awake, just waiting for you to slip up and do something wrong.

No wonder they want to hide!

But that's not the God I see in the Bible. It's certainly not the El Roi Hagar met in the desert or the God who spoke to me at the airport and sent me that gift of twenty cardinals.

No, the all-seeing God we encounter in the Bible is also a God who sees the entire universe through the eyes of love. Love, like light, is part of His very essence. The apostle John drives that reality home:

> Dear friends, let us *love* one another, for *love* comes from God. Everyone who *loves* has been born of God and knows God. Whoever does not *love* does not know God, because *God is love.…* No one has ever seen God; but if we *love* one another, God lives in us and his love is made complete in us.… And so we know and rely on the love God has for us. *God is love.* Whoever lives in love lives in God, and God in him.… We love because he first *loved* us.[18]

The message is powerfully clear: The God who sees you and me is, in fact, nothing less than Love itself.

David J. Abbott draws on Paul's famous "love passage" in 1 Corinthians 13 to show us exactly what that means.[19] You know the passage I'm talking about. It's the one that describes love as patient, kind, not envious or boastful or rude, and so on. I've always understood it to be a picture of the way we are supposed to love one another—and it is.

But Dr. Abbott points out that if God is love, all the characterstics outlined in 1 Corinthians 13 apply first of all to Him. In other words, 1 Corinthians 13 paints an intimate portrait of a God …

- *who is patient,* always willing to give a second chance … and a third, and a hundredth.[20]
- *who is kind,* treating us with sympathy and caring.[21]
- *who is not proud or boastful*—although He could be. Instead, He's gentle and humble.[22]
- *who is not easily angered*—and once we repent of our wrongs, He forgets about them completely.[23]
- *who rejoices in truth.* In fact, He *is* truth.[24]
- *who can be trusted.* He is faithful, and He never gives up. He will never let you down.[25]

That's love. That's God. And I don't know about you, but I find this whole idea immensely reassuring. There's no need to hide from such a loving God.

Even when we wonder if He can truly understand what it's like to be us.

the God who sees you ... really gets it

"You just don't get it!"

Ever hear that from the mouth of a teenager? Back when I had four of them in the house at once, I heard it a lot—often punctuated with the slam of a door or a toss of the head. My son and daughters all had times when they were convinced I had no clue what they were going through or what their lives were like.

And you know what? In a way, they were right. I *had* forgotten a lot about what it was like to be young—to obsess over grades, walk the popularity gauntlet at school, and experience my first heartbreak. Plus, some of the things my kids experienced were just not part of my world when I was their age. Drugs and alcohol did not figure into my daily school reality. I had no cell phone, no pressure to be bone thin, no parents walking through divorce. Internet porn didn't even exist when I was a kid.

The truth is, understanding what my kids' lives were like required a huge effort of imagination on my part, plus a fair amount of research. Sometimes I succeeded in "getting it," but often I didn't— and my kids knew that.

Have you ever felt that way about God? Have you ever suspected that He just doesn't get what it's like to be you?

It's one thing to be seen. It's another thing—a wonderful thing—to be loved. But can an all-powerful, purely good God truly appreciate what it's like to be human—subject to sin and sniffles, dirt and disease, pushed around by our hormones and our families, vulnerable to grief and pain?

Can a perfect Being understand what it's like to be far from perfect?

He certainly understands the limitations of our bodies because
He made us in the first place. "He knows our frame," the psalmist
insists. "He remembers that we are dust"—or, as Eugene Peterson
translates, "that we're made of mud."[26] God's well aware of our physical limitations, our emotional shortcomings, the way our histories
and our choices have limited or even crippled us. And somehow,
under it all, He sees potential.

But does God really understand what it's like to feel emotions?
Christians have disagreed on this since the earliest days of the
church. Some claim the Almighty is above all that, that He cannot
get truly angry or feel pain. But Dennis Ngien writes persuasively
that …

> if God is devoid of passions, we would have to
> rewrite the Bible. The Bible eloquently affirms that
> God can be wounded. In Hosea, for instance, God
> cries out about wayward Israel: "How can I give you
> up, Ephraim? How can I hand you over, O Israel?…
> My heart recoils within me; my compassion grows
> warm and tender. I will not execute my fierce anger;
> I will not again destroy Ephraim; for I am God and
> no mortal, the Holy One in your midst, and I will
> not come in wrath" (11:8–9 NRSV).
>
> God suffered the pain of the broken relation-
> ship with Israel, but … God's anger is not a childish
> loss of temper nor is it a frustrated love turned sour
> or vindictive. Rather, it is an expression of pure
> love that does not allow him to stand by idly in the

face of unrighteousness. God's true nature is active love; wrath is God's "strange work," which opposes anything that stands between God and us. Wrath is God's love burning hot in the presence of sin, proof that he cares.[27]

But God did so much more than understand our limitations and respond to us passionately. God actually chose to become human—which means He *really* gets it.

He actually put on skin and flesh and became what we are. We call it the incarnation. The coming of Jesus.

When God chose to be born on earth as Jesus, He accepted the reality of nerve endings. He learned what it was like to need sleep, to be hungry, to be lonely and disappointed. He experienced life through the five senses. He heard children laughing and maniacs screaming. He gazed at dancing flowers and leprous feet. He reveled in clean, smooth linen and felt the stab of thorns on His brow. He enjoyed the salty tang of fresh-caught fish and tasted vinegar from a sponge. He inhaled the smell of bread baking and the unmistakable stench of death.

Jesus laughed. He wept. He knew what it was like to live in a human family, to be held in a mother's arms and looked up to by little brothers and sisters and supported by loving friends. He also knew what it was like to be hated and rejected by others for doing good. He knew what it was like to feel forgotten and ignored and invisible.

And yes, He knew temptation, too. The Bible says Jesus was "tempted in every way, just as we are."[28] He knew what it was like to feel the pull of the flesh, to want to give in to selfishness or pride or lust or just plain weariness, to want to take the easy route instead of the right one. Even, perhaps, to be disobedient to His calling.

"Tempted," the Bible says, "in *every* way." Jesus' decision to turn away from temptation, to show the world it was possible to be human and not sin, came with a mighty struggle. He knows firsthand what it means to wrestle with weakness.

And if God didn't get suffering before the incarnation, He certainly understood it once He became human—even the special sting of undeserved suffering. Isaiah prophesied in painful detail what Jesus would go through:

> He was despised and rejected by men,
>   a man of sorrows, and familiar with suffering.
> Like one from whom men hide their faces
>   he was despised, and we esteemed him not.
>
> Surely he took up our infirmities
>   and carried our sorrows....
> He was pierced for our transgressions;
>   he was crushed for our iniquities ...
> though he had done no violence,
>   nor was any deceit in his mouth.[29]

Fear, anger, hunger, thirst, suffering, even death—because He chose to become human, God has experienced it all. He's the God who gets it, who can love us from a place of true understanding.

the God who sees you ... acts

But God doesn't stop there.

He doesn't just look at us with fondness or sympathize with our weakness. He gets involved. He actively pursues a relationship with us. Again and again, even when we don't know it, He intercedes on our behalf.

God sees our problems and helps us solve them. He notices our needs and moves to meet them. He's both willing to help and capable of helping. In fact, according to Isaiah 65:24, God starts responding even before we're finished crying out to Him. "Before they call I will answer," God says. "While they are still speaking I will hear."

At any given second, God is in the process of rescuing His messed-up creation ... which means you and me. Listen to His promise:

> Don't be afraid, I've redeemed you.
>> I've called your name. You're mine.
> When you're in over your head, I'll be there with you.
>> When you're in rough waters, you will not go down.
> When you're between a rock and a hard place,
>> it won't be a dead end—
> Because I am God, your personal God....
>> I paid a huge price for you....
> I'd sell the whole world to get you back,
>> trade creation just for you.[30]

Once again, that doesn't mean God always changes our circumstances or does what we want Him to do. He didn't do that with

Hagar, and many times He has not done that for me. Remember, God doesn't think the way we think—which means He often acts in ways we don't expect or even approve of.

Instead of rescuing us from our painful circumstances, for instance, He often uses those circumstances to strengthen us and mature us. Instead of solving our problems, He uses those problems to teach us patience and trust. Instead of rushing to our aid, He often makes us wait until the very last minute for our deliverance. We may not even know in this lifetime some of the things He has done to help us.

But that doesn't mean God expects us to stumble blindly through our lives without a sense of His presence. In fact, the very opposite is true. The God of the Bible is all about relationships. He created you and me for intimacy with Him—which means He *wants* to connect with us.

the God who sees you …
wants you to know Him

God didn't put us here on earth to play hide-and-seek, but to walk closely with Him and share in the unfolding of His kingdom. Yes, He can be mysterious. Yes, He can hide Himself. Yes, He often works in ways we don't understand. But He also takes great pains to show Himself to us—and the ways He does this are astonishing in their range and creativity.

- *God reveals Himself through His Word,* which in a sense is God's self-portrait. In the pages of the

Bible, we find a record of who He is, how He sees us, and what His intentions toward us are.

- *God also reveals Himself in His creation.* The beauty and power of nature tell us something about who He is—organized, immense yet intricate, awe-inspiring, bountiful, surprising, artful. "The heavens declare the glory of God," exults Psalm 19:1. And so do twenty cardinals in the snow!

- *God reveals Himself in our lives through epiphany revelations*—those moments when His Spirit opens our eyes and we suddenly see the world differently. When suddenly, somehow, we become aware of His presence and learn a little more about who He is.

- *God reveals Himself through small "coincidences"*—a check in the mail, an encouraging phone call, a comment from a stranger—that reassure us God is near. (I love Squire Rushnell's term for such little revelations: "godwinks."[31])

- *God reveals Himself in retrospect,* when we look back and realize how He has worked out a challenging or painful situation, and through memory, when we tell ourselves the story of what He has done for us in the past.

- *God reveals Himself through our faith,* which is a gift of the Holy Spirit, and through a simple sense of His presence, which is sometimes the greatest gift of all.

- *God reveals Himself in the gathered witness and fellowship of His people*—in worship, in sharing together, in prayers and the breaking of bread, and in the ways God's people care for one another.

- *God reveals Himself in the faces of those in need,* inviting us to see Him as we minister to the least of these who are His brothers and sisters.[32] In fact, this is where Jesus always insisted that we would see Him.

- *Most powerfully, God reveals Himself through Jesus,* who is "the image of the invisible God."[33] Jesus said it plainly: "If you've seen Me you've seen the Father."[34]

However God chooses to reveal Himself to us, we can know it's for our benefit. Because He is who He is—the unseen God who wants us to see Him, the all-seeing God who is working out the big picture, the loving God who understands our challenges and works in our behalf—we can trust Him. We can be ourselves with Him, knowing He sees us anyway and still loves us. And we can trust Him to show Himself to us in His own way and His own time, through His good and perfect gifts.

Because that's just the way He is.

chapter three

what God sees in you

O Lord, you have examined my heart
and know everything about me....
You know what I am going to say even before I say it, Lord.
You go before me and follow me.
You place your hand of blessing on my head.

Psalm 139:1, 4–5 NLT

There's a scene in the movie *The Joy Luck Club* that I have always found very moving. Based on a novel by Amy Tan, this film tells the story of four Chinese-born women and their American-born daughters.

One of the daughters, June, has always felt she's a disappointment to her mother, Suyuan, who suffered greatly as a young woman in China and made many sacrifices to give her daughter every advantage. June feels especially uncomfortable when compared to Waverly, the brilliant, confident, and highly successful daughter of Suyuan's best friend.

These feelings come to a head one evening at a dinner party where Suyuan serves her famous steamed crab dish. During the dinner, Waverly openly belittles June, and Suyuan fails to come to her daughter's defense. Later, when June and her mother are cleaning up in the kitchen, June finally blurts out her pain: "I'm just sorry that you got stuck with such a loser, that I've always been so disappointing…. My grades, my job. Not getting married. Everything you expected of me."

"Not expect anything," her mother answers. "Only hoping best for you. That's not wrong, to hope."

Then June's pain just overflows. "Well, it hurts. Because every time you hoped for something I couldn't deliver, it hurt. It hurt me, Mommy. And no matter what you hoped for, I'll never be more than what I am. And you never see that, what I really am."

Her mother just looks at her for a long minute, then removes a jade pendant from around her neck and hands it to her daughter. "June, since your baby time, I wear this next to my heart. Now you wear next to yours. It will help you know: I see you. I see you."

Then she goes on to talk about the dinner they just enjoyed: "That bad crab. Only you tried to take it. Everybody else want best quality. You, you thinking different. Waverly took best-quality crab. You took worst. Because you have best-quality heart. You have style no one can teach. Must be born this way."

She looks deep into her daughter's eyes and repeats: "I see you."[1]

And by that point, any mother would be weeping, any daughter moved—because that scene so beautifully depicts the transformative power of being seen. You can see it on June's face—the powerful internal shift as she begins to see herself and her relationships differently.

There's something about being seen, really seen, that changes everything, because it changes the way we see ourselves—just as knowing we are seen by God makes all the difference … unless we, like June, get the wrong idea about how our heavenly Parent looks at us.

It's so easy to do. We get mistaken ideas and feelings about what God expects of us and about the way we measure up to those expectations. And those mistaken ideas and feelings hurt us. We feel forgotten, or worthless, or like failures. We're sure we don't measure up, that we're not enough for God or anyone else. We may know we're loved and forgiven, but we still feel like a disappointment to God.

That's why we need the powerful message of how our heavenly Father really sees us. And that's what I want for you in this chapter—to open your eyes and your heart to the person God sees when He looks at you.

Because the more you come to see yourself through God's eyes, the closer you'll move toward becoming who you were really meant to be.

always on His mind

I've heard people say, "God has enough to worry about without paying attention to my little problems." ·

Don't believe it.

The "God is too busy" idea is a misconception that keeps us from understanding how God sees us. It assumes that God is limited in His attention span, His energy, His capacity for love. And everything I read in the Bible, everything I experience when I keep my spirit open to my heavenly Father, convinces me that's just not true.

God is God! He's perfectly capable of keeping the universe on course and still knowing and loving you intimately. Don't let yourself fall into the heresy that God is too busy or limited or indifferent to be concerned with you personally.

The Bible says specifically that the Lord is "mindful" of us.[2] That He remembers us always. That He watches over us tenderly and never slumbers or sleeps. I love the way Mary DeMuth describes this:

> As I go to sleep tonight, I'll be picturing God the Father looking down on me. He sees my feet dangle off the bed, so he lifts them up. Takes off my shoes. Places fuzzy socks on my feet because He knows how cold my feet get. Then smooths the covers over me, watching me as my breath moves in and out.[3]

Isn't that a beautiful picture of mindful care and devotion? We're talking about a God who knows what's going on with you 24-7. You're on His radar all the time. Even if no one else sees you, God does. In fact, He knows every detail about you. Like a doting mother or a passionate lover, He has you memorized. The Bible says God even keeps track of every single hair on your head.[4] So of course He knows about your food allergies and your tendency toward depression and your imperfect body. Even the things that annoy you about yourself or pose serious challenges are part of the entire package God sees and notices and loves.

I'm not saying it's necessarily God's will that you can never eat nuts or you spend Decembers in a funk or you can't find jeans that fit! But I am saying that God is intimately aware of *everything* about you—every detail.

You never stop being on His mind.

I came to understand this more completely recently because of a little experiment I tried while babysitting my grandson Cohen. I happened to be reading a passage from the book of Isaiah that speaks eloquently of God's mindfulness:

> I will not forget you!
> See, I have engraved you on the palms of my hands.[5]

I looked down at Cohen. And then, on a whim, I grabbed an indelible marker and wrote his name on my own palm. I would never have guessed how often during the next few days that I would look down and see that baby's name! I'd be reminded of how I love him, how special he is. Most of the time I'd take a quick moment to pray for him. He was constantly on my mind—just as each one of us is constantly on the mind of our heavenly Father.

the apple of His eye

But God doesn't just notice you. He doesn't just keep track of what you're doing. He also delights in you.[6] He truly thinks you're wonderful. He's proud of you.

Think of the implications of having a heavenly Father who sees you this way. He celebrates you and actually enjoys your company. He loves the sound of your voice, recognizes your walk, and chooses to be near you constantly. He loves to spend time with you and loves for you to spend time with Him, both alone and in the company of His other children.

And one of His great joys is to lavish wonderful gifts upon you and delight you with beauty. Warm sunshine. Cool breezes. The rustle of leaves and the sparkle of water and the blessing of family and friends. Your heavenly Father loves to "give good gifts"[7] to His children, to provide above and beyond what you would ever expect. Blessing you and helping you are a joy to Him. He loves to see you smile!

And this is crucial to remember: *There is nothing you can do to change the way God sees you.* Nothing you can do to make Him love you any less. When you rebel, when you forget Him, when you get lost or fail—He doesn't stop desiring you or delighting in you.

But that doesn't mean the God who delights in you is blinded by love.

Because the God who sees you, the God who delights in you, also sees you just the way you are.

the you beyond the spin

Here's something I'm finally getting through my head after all my years: *You can't spin God.*

You can't manipulate the way you come across to Him, putting a carefully calculated foot forward. You can't give Him a little bit of you and make it look good or acceptable and then tuck the rest away.

We all do that with other people. Some of us do it a lot. We manipulate the way we appear to people or even to ourselves, doing whatever we can to make ourselves look a little better than we are or a little more clever, a little more selfless or a little more cool. We may even "fess up" to a smaller sin in order to hide something even deeper.

Sometimes we do it on purpose. Sometimes we do it by reflex and don't even know what we're doing. All too often, we even manage to fool ourselves.

But none of that works with God because He sees beyond the spin. He looks right through the image you project to others and even—maybe especially—the lies you give yourself and the issues you may not recognize.

Right through to the person you really are.

"For God sees not as man sees," the Bible tells us, "for man looks at the outward appearance, but the LORD looks at the heart."[8]

That means there's no use even trying to pretend with Him. In fact, the more you pay attention to God and the closer you draw to Him, the more you'll learn about who you are and who you can be—because God sees your complete self and can reveal it to you. He can shine His light on the hurt places and the sin places, revealing in order to redeem and to heal.

Jesus did exactly that in the Gospels. He looked at people and cut through their hypocrisy, their self-protection, their fear and confusion and delusions. Again and again He put His finger not only on who they really were, but on what they needed most.

When the scribes and Pharisees tried to trick Him with their questions and accusations, He punctured their pretenses, revealing their pride and spiritual bankruptcy.[9]

When the rich young ruler asked what he needed to do about eternal life, Jesus cut right through to the man's weak spot: his materialistic values.[10]

When the Samaritan woman at the well misrepresented her family situation, He zeroed in on her brokenness, her loneliness, her troubled past. As she later related to her neighbors, He "told me everything I ever did."[11] Then He offered her what she needed most: the gift of Himself.[12]

And later, when Simon Peter loudly proclaimed His love and loyalty—"I'll never betray you!"—Jesus gently skewered his bravado and predicted His friend would do exactly what he never wanted to do.[13]

It's not a comfortable thing, being seen as we are, without spin, without pretense. It can be embarrassing, humiliating, even devastating. And some people, like the Pharisees, just can't take it. But being seen as we are can also be liberating, once we realize that the God who sees us as we are also loves us exactly as we are.

When we're so tired we can't think straight.

When we're worrying about finances or obsessing about a dinner that needs to go just right or so furious we just can't keep our mouths shut.

When we do a hard thing and fall on our face or want to do the right thing and don't quite manage it.

When we quietly serve others, then grumble because no one notices.

God sees it all. And none of it changes the way He looks at us.

Brennan Manning sums up this reality so beautifully:

> I am now utterly convinced that on Judgment Day,
> the Lord Jesus is going to ask each of us one ques-
> tion, and only one question: "Did you believe that
> I love you? That I desire you? That I waited for you
> day after day? That I long to hear the sound of your
> voice?… I know your whole life story. I know every
> skeleton in your closet. I know every moment of
> sin, shame, dishonesty, and degraded love that has
> darkened your past. Right now I know your shal-
> low faith, your feeble prayer life, your inconsistent
> discipleship. And My word is this: I dare you to
> trust that I love you just as you are and not as you
> should be.[14]

But does that mean that what we should be doesn't matter? Does
the God who sees us just overlook all those skeletons in our closets
and ignore all that "sin, shame, dishonesty, and degraded love"?

No, the God who sees everything about us loves you way too
much to look past the sin in our lives.

And believe it or not, that's good news.

why God hates your sin

Isn't that what we're all afraid of? Isn't that why we spend so much
time hiding in the shadows instead of living in the light? We don't

like the idea of being seen by God because, if we're honest with ourselves, we know we're seriously messed-up people. Our shortcomings are all too evident. We can't stop sinning. We're not even sure we *want* to stop sinning. And we're pretty sure God doesn't look kindly on all that sin.

We're right.

The Bible is pretty clear that God hates sin. That He judges our selfishness and rebellion. That He calls us to repent and commands us to "sin no more."[15]

But what we tend to forget is the *reason* that God hates our sin.

It's because He loves us so much.

Sin by definition is any thought or action that cuts us off from God. It has the potential to destroy us, and that's the very last thing God wants for us.

So yes, God sees your sin clearly and takes it very seriously. But He doesn't look at your sin like a sadistic schoolteacher wielding a red pen. He's not looking for ways to flunk you from your place in His kingdom. Instead, He agonizes over you like a loving parent who hates the way you're hurting yourself and others.

As the parent currently of three grown children and one teenager, I understand that distinction so well. There have been times in all my kids' lives when I have discovered a transgression on their part—a rule ignored, a promise broken, questionable behavior, downright rebellion. I've known what it is to drive through darkened neighborhoods in the middle of the night, searching for a wayward child who didn't come home.

Because I'm human, I have to admit that my children's poor choices have sometimes made me angry. I've responded in ways that were too controlling and sometimes less than loving. But I can honestly say that my dominant attitude toward my wayward children was love, not judgment. My primary motivation was to keep them from jeopardizing their relationships and their future.

As a parent, I took my children's transgressions *very* seriously. But I also saw beyond their transgressions to the persons I knew they were, the persons they could be, the persons I prayed they would choose to be.

And that, I believe, is the way your heavenly Father sees your sin—only much more purely, more perfectly. He takes your sin seriously, but He also sees beyond it. Like a good parent, He will let you suffer the consequences of your actions, but He doesn't condemn you. Instead, He offers you a way to move past the sin in your life. He offers the gifts of forgiveness and redemption. And He never, ever gives up on you.

But keep in mind that God doesn't *only* see sin when He looks at you. He doesn't just focus on what you do wrong. He also notices—and celebrates—what you do right.

your best audience

Did you ever see the television show *Undercover Boss,* which premiered in early 2010? It's a reality show that follows the heads of companies who go "undercover" in their own companies. The CEOs or other high-ranking executives disguise themselves and join the ranks of ordinary employees—scrubbing toilets, assembling burgers, loading trucks, cleaning motel rooms, and getting to know their fellow workers. Usually they struggle to keep up with the work, and they gain new appreciation for what these jobs entail. They also come to appreciate the hardworking, creative, enthusiastic employees who struggle to do a good job while coping with money woes, medical problems, and other personal issues.

At the end of all the shows, the undercover bosses reveal their true identities and express verbal appreciation along with more tangible rewards—bonuses, vacations, promotions. Tears flow at these "reveals." But it's not the tangible rewards that touch the employees most deeply. *What matters most to them is realizing their efforts have been noticed.*

There's power in those tearful moments because they touch us where we all live. We work so hard and pour out our lives and mean so well, and too often we feel that nobody notices what we do. Perhaps nobody even cares.

But God does.

Matthew 6:4 says it clearly: "Then your Father, who sees what is done in secret, will reward you."

Since God sees what is secret, that means He's well aware of what nobody else even notices. He sees your faithfulness and your obedience, even in the face of doubts. He sees the choices you make to follow Him and persevere in doing right. He sees you trying again, even when you're weary. And because God looks at the heart, I believe He sees and honors your attitudes and your good intentions, even when you don't quite succeed. He honors your attempts to act on what you hear Him saying, even when you get the message wrong. He even honors your honest doubt and your feeble attempts to move toward Him despite those doubts.

In fact, just as Jesus held out His hand to a sinking Peter on the lake,[16] God responds to your smallest attempt to reach Him. He sees what you're trying to do and reaches down His hand to help you up.

I truly hope that you receive approval and appreciation for what you work to accomplish here on earth. I hope you enjoy the satisfaction of knowing your efforts are successful and appreciated. But even when you feel like nobody sees you, keep reminding yourself that God does. In fact, He's your best and most appreciative audience.

When you take a step of obedience and faithfulness, He's applauding all the way.

the *real* you

John Eldredge writes, "You are not what you think you are. There is a glory to your life that your Enemy fears, and he is hell-bent on destroying that glory before you act on it.... But once you begin to see with [God's] eyes, once you have begun to know [the truth] from the bottom of your heart, it will change everything."[17]

Stop. Read that again. Ponder the power of this truth.

You were created in God's image, with a glory that reflects His own glory. God made you to be His, He claims you for His own, and every time He looks at you He sees a reflection of Himself. A unique personality, incomparably beautiful. Created out of love and for love. Made to live forever. That's your spiritual essence, your true self. And that's who God sees when He looks at you. Not just your sins and shadows. Not just your feeble efforts to do right. Not just the intimate details of the earthly you. But the *real* you. The eternal you.

God and the story of your life

It's so hard for us to really see ourselves. We compare our weaknesses to other people's strengths, our strengths to another's weakness. We judge ourselves too leniently or too strictly. We beat ourselves up for things we can't control but excuse ourselves for actions we could avoid if we really wanted to.

It's also difficult for us to understand what has happened to us in the past. How our upbringing has shaped us. How trauma has wounded us. How our own sin and the sin of others has marked us. How God's grace has kept us from catastrophe and made up for what we lacked. It's true that we can often see more clearly when looking back, but not always. Memory is notoriously unreliable, and some puzzles are never solved.

And as for the future—do you know what you really want? I've often had a hard time understanding that for myself. I find it difficult to distinguish between what I really need and what I lust after, my God-given "heart desires" and my own selfish wants.

Amid all this confusion, it's an absolute gift for me to remember that the God who sees me is the God who knows "the end from the beginning."[18] Remember, God is Lord of the past, the present, and the future. So when He looks at you, He sees the entire story of who you are and where you've been.

He understands what you've been through, the forces that have shaped you and made you ... you. He considers your family history, the people who raised you, taught you, loved you, failed you. He recognizes the traumas that mark you and echo in your memory. He sees the love and support, the misunderstandings and broken relationships, the successes and failures. All the unique combinations of events and experiences that have brought you to this current moment are an open book to God when He looks at you.

God also sees your present circumstances—where you live, who you share your life with, what your days are like, the secrets you don't dare tell anyone. He's aware of your daily needs for sustenance, your deeper needs for meaning and involvement, your longings and dreams and desires. He sees what you go through when it's just one thing after another, when the bottom drops out, when a straw breaks the camel's back, when you're holding on to sanity by the skin of your teeth. He understands what helps you, what holds you back, what still has the potential to waylay you in the future.

More important, when He sees you, He doesn't leave you there. He's a God who acts, remember?

He sees your weariness ... and offers you His strength.

He sees your feelings of inadequacy—such a common experience with women—and offers you His completeness.

He sees your pain ... and suffers beside you.

He sees your doubt ... and gives you reason to trust Him.

He sees your worry and your anger ... and offers you peace.

He sees your small steps of obedience ... and cheers you on.

He sees you stumble ... and helps you back on your feet.

He sees your loneliness ... and offers you His presence.

In all your daily needs (even those you don't know you have), He provides for you appropriately, often in ways you would never expect. And He longs for you to avail yourself of His provision.

The longer I live, the more I'm convinced that God never looks away from what we're going through. He is the God who suffers and rejoices with us on a daily basis. He sees it all clearly—even when we don't.

Simply put, God sees you with a depth and breadth that only He can. He sees how all the messy loose ends of your life weave together, how you can be whole.

One day, He promises, you will see it all too.

In the meantime, He's holding your future in His capable hands.

a special future

I began this book with a story of loneliness, doubt, and a family in disarray—the agonizing season of my divorce and its aftermath. God ministered to me sweetly through that time, assuring me in many ways that He did see me and was working in my life to bring about my future. But I never, ever thought it would include a man like Jerry … and a new marriage.

I had known Jerry for years, though not well. He was a widower who had experienced his share of trauma, including the long illness of his wife and sudden profound deafness in his fifties. He is older than I am and not really what I normally would have considered a good match. I'm pretty sure that I, with my rambunctious house-hold, was not exactly his type either! But at some point after my divorce was final, when I was struggling to rebuild my life and raise my kids, Jerry quietly and respectfully proclaimed his intentions to be there for me, to be my friend, and eventually, when I was ready, to make me his wife.

It took a while for me to be ready. I take marriage seriously, and after the trauma of my divorce I was wounded and gun-shy. But Jerry persisted, in his gentle way. Finally I agreed to marry him. And what a spectacular unexpected blessing that man has been in my life and in the lives of my children. Not only has he seen me dancing beyond so many circumstances; he has also *helped* me dance. Most important, he is my loving, encouraging partner as I attempt to respond to God's calling and move into the special future I believe He has in store for me.

He has a future for you as well.

"For I know the plans I have for you," says the Lord in a famous verse from the book of Jeremiah. "They are plans for good and not for disaster, to give you a future and a hope."[19]

"No one's ever seen or heard anything like this," adds the apostle Paul, echoing the prophet Isaiah, "never so much as imagined anything quite like it—what God has arranged for those who love him."[20]

He sees what you were made to be and what you can be. He's committed to walking you through your troubles. He's planning to fulfill your deepest needs, grant the "desires of your heart,"[21] and guide you through and beyond your troubles. He has reserved a place for you in His life and His kingdom, both here on earth and in eternity. Gently and with grace, He's constantly in the process of positioning you where you need to be.

That's another reason He takes your sins so seriously: so you can be set free from their burden and live more fruitfully. That's why He stresses obedience and listening: so He can put you in the right place at the right time. That's why He disciplines you and teaches you: so you'll be ready for your assigned role in His kingdom.

What God has in mind for you is as individual as you are. And our infinitely creative, inventive, redemptive God is always at work using the raw materials of your life to work out His plan.

When I look back over my own life, I'm astounded by the ways God has used my gifts, my talents, my decisions, my life circumstances, even my mistakes to put me exactly where He wanted.

My older sister's interest in adoption, my experiences as a flight attendant, and my former husband's international travel all came together to shape my current family and my career.

My parents' hospitable hearts and my growing interest in the "art and soul" of hospitality eventually led to a speaking focus, a business, a cookbook, and some of my dearest friendships.

My struggles as a single mom gave me a heart for those in similar circumstances, a very personal ministry to those I consider modern-day widows and orphans.

Even the darkest moment of my life—a painful and lingering depression—became a tool God used to move me toward my future and hope.

Your story, of course, will be different from mine—constructed by God from the raw materials of your own life and your response to God's calling. But you can be confident that when God looks at you, He sees you dancing beyond your circumstances, whatever they are—living the life He has already prepared for you. He will put you where you need to be ... if you pay attention and obey His call.

But what if you don't obey? What if you rebel or lose your nerve or just don't understand what He's trying to do? I know there have been times in my life when I have done all three. And while I don't understand all the ways God works, I have come to believe these things with all my heart:

Nothing can happen to us that the Father is not aware of.

Nothing can happen to us that He can't use to further His kingdom.

We can pull away from God. We can try to hide from Him. We can even make choices that separate us from Him forever.

But none of this stops God from looking at us through the eyes of love. And none of it will delay the coming of His kingdom.

I believe that God has a plan for your life, a specific place for you in His future. But I also believe that the specific unfolding of God's plan is fluid and subject to change. God, like a Master Artist, adjusts His plan as we make our choices in life. When we smudge the painting, He works our smudge into the master design, using even our sins and our mistakes for His purposes.

If you keep your focus on God, He will put you exactly where you need to be. But even if you lose focus, if you're disobedient and lose your way, you can turn back to Him and still trust Him to use all your pain and mistakes to put you where you need to be.

God is infinitely creative, infinitely willing to go to whatever lengths to help you dance beyond your circumstances into His future. And He does it because of the way He sees you. Because ...

you're worth it!

This to me is the heart of the gospel, the heart of what God sees in you. When the God of the universe looks at you, He sees someone who is infinitely worth all His love and time and trouble. Someone who is:

- worth trying again and again to reach.
- worth teaching, even when you're stubborn or rebellious or don't get it.
- worth disciplining, even when you resist.
- worth waiting faithfully for—as the father waited for the prodigal son.[22]
- worth seeking out—as the shepherd searched for his lost sheep.[23]
- worth the trouble of redeeming.
- worth forgiving, again and again.
- worth dying for.

Because He really does see you—your past, your present, your possibilities. He is painfully aware of your sins and your failures but also rejoices over your hidden good deeds and your best intents. He cherishes your true self—the spark of divine in you—and delights in your human particularity. He sees you accurately, from the inside out. And you are enough for Him, just as you are.

If you have trouble believing that, look at the facts:

As the Father, He made you and adopted you into His family.[24]

As the Son, He thought you were worth dying for.

As the Spirit, He chooses to live within you.

As the Alpha and Omega, the beginning and the end, He sees for you a role in His ever-unfolding story.

chapter four

choosing a miracle

Open your mouth and taste, open your eyes and see—
how good GOD is.

Psalm 34:8 MSG

For ten years I lived in the shadow of Pikes Peak. I had an enviable view of that beautiful mountain from the back deck of my home. And in those ten years, I found myself constantly amazed by the way that monumental pile of rock could completely disappear.

One day I'd look out the sliding glass doors and almost be overwhelmed by the sight of Pikes Peak in all its glory—gleaming in the sunlight, dominating the view.

The next day—or even the next hour—the clouds would roll in, and there would be no trace of a mountain. Seriously! You'd never even know it was there. If I invited a new friend outside to enjoy our beautiful view of Pikes Peak, she'd laugh. There was literally nothing to see but the trees and grass of our very ordinary backyard.

The mountain, of course, was there all along. It never moved.

What changed was our ability to perceive it.

I don't know about you, but there are plenty of times when I just can't see God—not physically, of course, but not in a spiritual sense either. I can't hear or perceive Him. I look around, and it's as if He's just not there.

I know I love God. I believe He's with me, and I want to trust what I know. Yet there are still so many times I find myself God-blind and God-deaf—unable to sense His presence. I stare out into my ordinary life and see nothing but … my ordinary life.

How can I believe God sees me if I can't see Him?

The testimony of Hagar is that we *can* "see" the God who sees us. We can be aware of His presence, of what He is doing in the world and our lives. That's the testimony of the Bible. And even though I've spent my share of days squinting into the fog, it's my testimony too.

We *can* see God.

But sometimes it takes a miracle.

the miracle of a perspective change

Several years ago I conducted a television interview with a man who was struggling with cancer. I asked him a fairly typical Christian interview question: "Are you trusting God for a miracle?" And I have never forgotten his reply: "I've learned that sometimes the greatest miracle is just a perspective change."

That man said a lot of insightful things that day, but that one phrase kept echoing in my mind. It's still echoing, in fact, because it has proven true so often in my life. I've learned never to underestimate the power of changing the way I see. And I've come to believe that often in our lives, we won't be able to perceive the God who sees us until we're willing to see things differently.

I believe it's perfectly possible to spend an entire lifetime looking at ordinary things and events—family, friends, fear, and disappointments—and never have the smallest hint that God is there or that He is active in our lives. It's easy. Happens all the time.

It's possible to look back on a life—all the things that have happened up till now—and not see any kind of pattern. It's also possible to look into the future and see more of the same. It's even possible to have an occasional glimpse into another dimension, a one-time spiritual awakening, then lapse back into the ordinary and never really be changed.

But here's the alternative: We can *choose* to spend life in the same circumstances, the same places, among all the same people, and continually be struck by the wonderful truth that God is there, that He's in control, that He loves us and is aware of us and wants us to be part of what He's doing in the world.

There's a kind of miracle, in other words, that we can choose.

We can choose the miracle of a perspective change.

choosing and being chosen

Does that mean that seeing God is just a matter of personal choice?

Not exactly.

It's always a little difficult to sort out what we can choose and what we can't choose in this life. Theologians have been trying to sort it out for centuries, juggling concepts of God's sovereignty and human free will, delving into the mysteries of what is up to us and what is up to God.

It's a mystery, a paradox—that God is in control of the entire universe, yet He gives us freedom of will. And that paradox is fully in play when it comes to seeing God.

Because ultimately, it is God's choice to reveal Himself to us.

But we must choose to see what God reveals. We must have what the Bible calls eyes to see and ears to hear and a heart to perceive.[1]

the gift of epiphany

God's appearances are never command performances—at least, we're not the ones who can command them. Our ability to perceive Him is always a gift. He initiates those moments when, for no reason we can fathom, the veil that keeps us from seeing the unseen realm is pulled aside. The clouds lift from the mountain. Our perspective shifts, and we *see* things the way they really are. What seemed distant or theoretical seems suddenly real. Or we suddenly *know* something to be true that we could never even have imagined.

I think, for instance, of the disciples on the mountain, fighting fatigue, struggling unsuccessfully to be faithful to their Lord and keep their heavy eyelids open. Then suddenly, without warning, catching a vision of Jesus in His transfigured glory along with Moses and Elijah. What an amazing shift of perception. No wonder Peter didn't want to come down off that mountain or let go of that moment.[2]

Or I think of Saul on the road to Damascus, being knocked off his donkey by a light so brilliant it blinded him ... and changed forever the way he saw the world and, quite frankly, himself.[3]

Has anything like that ever happened to you? You might not have seen a light or experienced a vision. But maybe you've had one of those moments when everything seems to come clear and you suddenly understand reality in a whole new way. When you find yourself newly and intensely aware of God's presence. When you are granted the gift of peering past the veil and you just *know* you've encountered the God who sees you. Something clicks in your mind and soul and spirit, and you suddenly think, *Yes!*

As I mentioned in chapter 2, that's called an *epiphany* moment. And if it has ever happened to you, you know what a true miracle it can be.

It happened to me just recently, while I was sitting in the car with my daughter Mackenzie. Actually, the whole thing started several hours earlier, when I realized with a start that it was December 22 and I hadn't even begun to get ready for Christmas.

This was not normal for me. For years I have loved everything about preparing for Christmas. Multiple trees in my house. Candles everywhere. Parties all through December. Piles of presents under the tree, and amazing food on the table. But this year, Christmas had sort of been pushed aside by a family wedding. All my energy had been focused on getting my daughter Tatiana married to her Ben.

There had been showers and shopping, wedding gifts to buy and wrap, people coming into town, and decorations to put up. I'd catered a rehearsal dinner for sixty people and made the appetizers for the reception. Our house had been turned into a big bed-and-breakfast for visiting family and friends.

It had also been a highly emotional experience—because that's the way weddings are, and because weddings where divorce, remarriage, and adoption are involved can push the drama off the charts. The ceremony had been beautiful, the fellowship sweet. But I couldn't ever remember feeling quite so weary or emotionally drained—not to mention financially depleted.

And now, I suddenly realized, I had only forty-eight hours to make Christmas happen—shopping, wrapping, cooking, everything. I was feeling like a failure before I even started.

That's when Mackenzie called. "Mom, I've got to go to Target this morning. Do you have time to go with me?"

Yes! I thought. *Perfect timing.* I could take care of my to-do list and have some much-needed time with my firstborn. My efficient, get-it-done mode kicked in as I grabbed a large coffee, picked up my shopping list, and headed for Target with Mackenzie.

Would you believe I got all the shopping done in less than an hour? (That's one upside of a limited budget.) I stuffed all my packages in the car, and we started for home, my mind already racing ahead to what I needed to do next.

But then, as we drove, I fell into a conversation with Mackenzie. She shared some ideas she'd been writing about in her blog—thoughts about her experience of being an adult child from a divorced family, about taking responsibility for her life, and about the meaning of Christmas. Her insights were profound, thoughtful, seasoned with both pain and maturity. And by the time we pulled up in my driveway, time had stilled. All my concerns about shopping and cooking and making Christmas happen had faded.

"Mom," Mackenzie said to me there in the car, "Christ came when we didn't acknowledge Him, when we weren't grateful, when we were blind to our need and determined to have our own way. He came when we didn't think we needed Him. And Mom, I am learning that He still comes, no matter what. He comes to free us from the failure of our lives, from the broken promises that seem to define us. He says, 'I saw you in your need. And I still see you. I am restoring all you thought was lost, all you have grieved and left behind. For with Me, all things are new.'"

I am fully convinced I experienced a miracle that morning through the life of my young adult daughter. With her words, with who she is, Mackenzie unwrapped my Christmas gift from the God who sees me. She helped me shift my perspective from anxiety over what needed to happen to peace over what God has done in all our lives.

"Well, we can take the tree down now, because Christmas has already happened," I told Jerry when I walked into the house that day. Jerry smiled when I explained what had happened in the car. "Christmas is more than what hangs on that tree," he said. "*He* hung on the tree. *He* is the gift."

Jesus gave and still gives us the miracle of a perspective change. Right in the middle of the messiness of life, He still comes. He still reveals Himself to our longing eyes.

choosing a miracle

And here's where the choice comes in.

That moment of epiphany was truly a gift to me. It came to me unbidden, a true gift of God—to my mind, as much a miracle as a healing of the body or a calming of the waters. I wasn't looking for it. I could not have manufactured that moment or forced it to happen.

And yet I still had a choice to make. I had to choose to *receive* the gift of that perspective change, to accept the reality that God really did see me and was intimately involved in every detail of my life. I had to step up to the reality that God was there in the very midst of my crazy life—when I was a young mom with four kids under five; when I was a single mom with four teenagers; when I was an exhausted, depleted, distracted woman with nothing done two days before Christmas.

I had to choose to have eyes to see and ears to hear and a heart to perceive Him when He chose to reveal Himself.

Choosing a perspective change is not just a matter of saying yes at the moment of revelation. There are also choices we can make that make us more *likely* to experience God in our day-to-day lives. Here are just a few that have made a difference to me and to others I have known.

choice #1: admit your blindness

So much goes on in our lives that we just don't see. That we *can't* see. That we don't want to see. That we're too busy to notice, too fearful to admit to ourselves, too wrapped up in one agenda or another to perceive. The simple fact that we're human, trapped in flesh and blood, makes it difficult for us to perceive what is beyond the reach of our senses.

Sometimes we're acutely aware of our blindness. Other times we haven't a clue. No wonder we have trouble seeing the God who sees us.

But here's the thing to remember: *Jesus healed the blind*. He opened the eyes of those who were physically sightless. And He healed—or tried to heal—those who just couldn't see what was in front of their faces. He told His disciples clearly:

> I don't want Isaiah's forecast repeated all over again:
>> Your ears are open but you don't hear a thing.
>>> Your eyes are awake but you don't see a thing.
>> The people ... stick their fingers in their ears
>>> so they won't have to listen;
>> They screw their eyes shut
>>> so they won't have to look,
>>> so they won't have to deal with me face-to-face
>>> and let me heal them.
> But you have God-blessed eyes—eyes that see! And God-blessed ears—ears that hear![4]

"God-blessed" eyes and ears—that's what God wants to give us. Healthy eyes and ears that can perceive what He is doing in the world. He wants to heal us. But He won't do that until we face up to the reality that *without* His healing touch, we're basically blind as bats.

There are a million aspects of our human experience that keep us blind—including the fact that God sometimes chooses to hide Himself from us. We'll explore some of these reasons in the next chapter. But no matter what causes it, we don't have to be as blind as we are—if we humbly admit our blindness and ask for healing. We can pray specifically, in the words of the song, "Open my eyes,

Lord." In my experience, the very act of humbly asking improves my ability to see.

While we're at it, we can choose to use what vision we do have. Because we have a much better chance of seeing the God who sees us if we're actually looking for Him.

choice #2: know where to look

Back in the first chapter, I said most of us are hide-and-seek creatures. And that's not a good thing when we're hiding out of fear and shame. But there's a healthy variety of hide-and-seek that has nothing to do with fear and shame and everything to do with the joy of finding one another and being found. I experience that every time I play the game with Cohen. He hides, and I hunt and hunt while he giggles in his (usually obvious) hiding place. I pretend I can't see him, then I make a big production of finding him, and we both laugh. Then it's my turn to hide and enjoy both his search for me and the fun of being found.

I can almost imagine God feeling the same kind of joy when He's hiding in places where He should be easy to find, the places where He told us from the beginning that He would be. He's given lots of hints about where He can be found—in the Bible, in the person of Jesus, in creation, in the faces of the needy, in the pattern and timing of events. Those are the first places to go if we want to see the God who sees us. But I would suggest you pay close attention to your own experience as well. If you want to see God, why not deliberately put yourself in the places where you tend to notice Him?

If it's in nature, take yourself to nature. Make time for a hike in the mountains, a bike ride along the lakeshore, an hour in your backyard observing the birds. And take yourself there with the explicit purpose of meeting God. Go there with God on your mind.

If God tends to speak to you in the act of creating or appreciating beauty, take yourself there, too. Take your sketchbook to a museum, your journal to the park, your breadboard to the kitchen, your rear end to the piano bench. But purpose your visit—choose to focus these creative times on seeking God so that your creative endeavor or appreciation becomes almost an act of prayer.

See my point? The list could go on and on. If you tend to feel close to God in church, go to church. (Okay, you should probably go to church anyway!) If it's with children, make a point to be around children. If you notice Him better in the wee hours of the morning or the middle of the night, get up and meet Him then.

Scripture says, "Seek the LORD while He may be found."[5] But I think we should also seek Him *where* He is often found. And then, when you find Him, enjoy the joyful presence of the God who sees you … and *wants* to be found.

choice #3: see God in everything

Don Osgood's experience with looking for God began in the hospital where his son was dying of cancer. His father was dying too, of the same type of cancer. It was one of those nightmare times in life when all existence seems to revolve around sterile rooms and beeping equipment, when the nurses and doctors and even the maintenance staff become almost as familiar as friends and family.

One day during that strange time, one of the hospital maintenance men shared a sentence that would change Don's life. The man told him simply, almost out of the blue, "See God in everything." And as Don Osgood explains it, his life began to change as he began to "look at even the simplest events of life with new recognition."[6]

"See God in everything." That's a critical choice when it comes to the miracle of a perspective change. And it's really not one choice, but a series of choices. A path. A journey. A way of life. A lifelong and deliberate search. It involves the cultivation of a deliberate kind of seeing.

You see, it's one thing to seek God. It's another thing to *recognize* God when you find Him. That's why it's so important to stretch our "seeing" muscles, to practice recognizing the many unexpected ways we may encounter God. Because while God has indeed told us where to look for Him, He also delights in surprising us in a multitude of ways. So we must become accustomed to the unaccustomed ways that God chooses to show Himself to us. We must be on a constant search for ways He's revealing Himself.

In Don Osgood's case, the search to see God in everything led him to support his wife in her quest to be a minister, even though she changed dramatically in the process and he feared losing her. The search led him to take his aged mother on one last adventure and then to take a prolonged train trip across the country. It led him to offer a home to a mentally ill girl and eventually to write a book or two. Each stop along the way, he encountered new ways of seeing God.

My journey has been completely different, but it's resulted in surprise encounters as well. I've seen God in the faces of my children—two born from my body and two brought to me from across two different oceans. I've met God at the end of my rope, when I was battling depression and anxiety. I have seen God provide financially, again and again, when all I could feel was fear. I have seen the reality of God doing the highly unexpected in very mundane and predictable circumstances.

Your quest to see God in everything will undoubtedly take a different direction as well. But it's not the particulars that matter—it's that choice to see God in all of it. Moment by moment, hour by hour, day by day, in the midst of our ordinary everydays and our disrupted weeks and months, our boredom and our stress, you *can* choose to have eyes to see and ears to hear and a heart to perceive what God is revealing to you—that He is indeed with you, that He sees you, that He wants you to know Him.

Because that's the secret, of course. We can choose to see God in everything … because wherever we look, God is there.

choice #4: believe to see

You've heard the old saying, "Seeing is believing." And that's probably true to some extent, though in this digital age we're more aware than ever of the way our eyes can be fooled and manipulated. Sadly, we can't always believe what we see.

But the longer I live, the more I'm convinced that the reverse of that saying really is true: "Believing is seeing." If you actually believe that something's out there, you're a lot more likely to be able to find it. Faith, in other words, is a crucial component in being able to see God in everything.

A simple example: Let's say my youngest daughter, Mikia, needs some poster board for a school project and asks me if we have any. I'm momentarily confused because I can't really remember. Then a lightbulb flashes—I remember buying some poster board for a speaking event, and I'm almost positive I have some left over. But where did I put it? I have to do some searching, but my belief that we actually have some of the poster board helps a lot. Instead of wasting time running to the store, I can eliminate that option and search in the places where I commonly keep poster board.

All right, that's a *really* simple example. But it highlights a serious spiritual reality: Once we choose to trust that God is near and wants to reveal Himself to us, we'll find it a lot easier to see Him at work in our lives. We'll notice the evidence more readily. We'll pick up on the little "coincidences" that offer reassurance and confirmation. Believing acts as a filter to help us interpret our experience and recognize what God might be doing in it.

Adopting an attitude of "believing is seeing" is not the same thing as seeing things just because you want them to be true. That's wishful thinking at best and mental illness at worst! It's also not a matter of making up your mind once and for all on all matters and never letting it change. That's stubbornness and rigidity.

"Believing is seeing" simply means recognizing that if we wait for *all* the evidence to come in before we decide to live in faith, we might never get around to actually living—and that trusting in our own (blind) understanding isn't all that dependable, either. It's a matter of hammering out a belief system that is meaningful and sustainable—supported by Scripture, by consistent experience, and by the witness of others—and then choosing to base our perspectives on these bedrock beliefs. Once we do that, we'll find it easier to shift our attitudes:

- from anxiety to trust.
- from fear to faith.
- from rebellion to acceptance.
- from impatience to watchful waiting.
- from apathy to expectation.

We know that such an attitude shift is possible because Jesus told us to do it. He encouraged us not to be anxious or afraid, to watch and wait for what the Lord was going to do.[7] Would He tell us to do all that if it's impossible?

choice #5: pay attention

Now we're getting into the "how to" of seeing God—choices we can make to set ourselves up for a shift in perspective. And this is the most basic of those choices: *We have to pay attention.* We have to be awake and aware, alert to what is happening both in the world around us and in our own inner world, resisting the temptation to numb out, to get lazy, to be so distracted by our own needs and what is happening around us that we lose sight of what God is doing.

Those are powerful temptations, as Jesus' disciples learned. He was always taking them along when He withdrew to be with His Father. He was continually asking them to stay awake and watch with Him, wait with Him. And what did they do consistently? You guessed it—they fell asleep!

Jesus did understand. He was human, remember, so He knew how strong the pull of the flesh could be. "The spirit is willing," He observed ruefully when the disciples had dozed off once again, "but the body is weak."[8] But Jesus also pleaded with them to keep trying. And He warned in a parable about the importance of staying alert over the long haul, watching and waiting attentively for God to show Himself.[9]

I believe that's what He calls us to today—to pay attention, to stay alert, to notice as much as we can—in our daily activities, in our prayer times, in every part of our lives. To consciously tune our physical senses as well as our spiritual awareness and continually watch for signs of God's presence. Because, as Kimberlee Conway Ireton so beautifully reminds us,

> I've found ... that the more closely I attend to the world around me—noticing the curve of my son's smile, the particular pitch of my daughter's voice, the even rhythm of the cat's breathing as he lies beside me on the sofa, the slant of sunshine on the dining room wall, the bright purple berries on a bush outside my window, the joyful bark of my husband's laugh—the more likely I am to receive a glimpse of the glory beyond this world.

> For in sharpening our physical senses to be more aware of this world, we are also quickening our spirits ... so that we will be more ready to receive visions of the unearthly beauty that lies just beyond our senses.[10]

choice #6: focus

It's a beautiful idea, isn't it—paying attention? Staying alert to the present moment. Watching and waiting. Noticing as much as we can.

But be honest. Does all that stuff about staying awake make you a little bit weary ... like it's just one more thing you still have to do?

The truth is, paying attention can wear us out. But that's because we lose sight of another reality—which is that we're not called to pay attention to *everything* all the time. We're only called to notice what's truly important.

And we'll only begin to get a feel for that when we learn to *focus*.

Focus in life is a little like turning the dials on a pair of binoculars or a telescope or a camera. You try to tune out whatever is extraneous, whatever makes the picture fuzzy. To focus is to concentrate, to ignore and eliminate distractions and hone in on the central object. To focus is to let the most important item loom large and everything else fade away.

And how do you learn how to focus on God? To me, the key is found in one of Jesus' most famous statements on seeing God: "Blessed are the pure in heart, for they will see God."[11]

There's been a lot written on what it means to be pure in heart. It certainly suggests being clean, coming to Jesus for forgiveness. It suggests singleness of motive, placing first things first. It makes me think of that other enigmatic statement of Jesus, translated in the King James Version as "when thine eye is single, thy whole body also is full of light."[12]

But to me, being pure in heart also involves being in the moment—fully alive, fully aware, completely honed in on what matters most. Not distracted by the past or the future, not distracted by guilt or shame, not imposing my own expectations, but just fixing my eyes on the things of God. Sitting at His feet and gazing up in adoration. Paying attention to the most important things.

That's exactly what Jesus told Martha of Bethany when she complained to Him about how hard she was working while her sister just sat at Jesus' feet. He said, "Martha, Martha ... you are worried and upset about many things, but *only one thing* is needed. Mary has chosen what is better, and it will not be taken away from her."[13]

"You're so concerned about all those other things," He was saying, "but I'm here with you right now, and that won't always be the case. Set aside all those things you're worrying about, and pay attention to the one thing that really matters."

"One thing"—that's focus. When we make that choice, we move closer to seeing the God who sees us. And interestingly enough, we don't lose sight of other things. We're still aware of what is around us—the beauty of nature, the wonder (and annoyance) of other people, the work we have to do, the delights and challenges of every day. The difference is that all those other things fall into their proper place. When we choose to focus on God, everything else takes on its proper perspective.

But we'll never be able to make that choice until we learn to do something else.

To be still.

choice #7: be still

My wonderful husband, Jerry, teaches me so much about God's heart on a daily basis, and he taught me another lesson just the other morning.

It was going to be a ridiculously busy day. My to-do list was a mile long, with errands and conference calls and deadlines, and I was already going a million miles an hour before my feet hit the floor. Coffee first, throw in a load of clothes, then up to the bathroom to shower and get dressed. I had just started putting on my makeup when Jerry walked into the adjacent bedroom and sat down quietly on the bed. He didn't say anything, just watched me while I was fluttering around, rubbing in lotion, swiping on mascara, doing my hair.

After a few minutes, I found myself getting a little irritated. Did he need something? Couldn't he see I was *very* busy today?

He still didn't say anything, just sat there quietly.

Finally, I stopped what I was doing and turned to him, brush in hand: "What—?"

He just looked at me in that gentle way he has and said, "Good morning."

And of course I melted. I put down my brush and went over to him, and we shared a delicious, calming hug. And I thought—not for the first time—that this man had shared the Father's heart with me, reminding me that I just can't connect with God unless I can stop fluttering. Stop rushing around. Stop all my busyness for even a moment.

Just … stop.

I'll never see the God who sees me unless I learn to be still.

And that's such a challenge for me. Perhaps the hardest of all for most of us.

We've all heard that psalm that tells us, "Be still, and know that I am God."[14] But flip that phrase around, and the message is even stronger:

Don't be still—*don't* know God.

And why is that? Simply because all the noise distracts us. All our frantic busyness pulls our attention away from what is real and important. All our rushing around keeps us from noticing that the Creator of the universe is right there beside us, waiting for us to stop fluttering and realize He's waiting.

It takes stillness for us to see Him, to recognize Him, to focus on Him. It takes silence. It takes shutting off the car, shutting off the music, shutting off the TV and the computer, shutting off the smartphone, shutting off the voices—all that external noise. And, though it's more difficult, shutting off the internal noise as well—the voices of our past, the curses that people have spoken over us, the lies whispered in our hearts, the confusion of others' expectations. We must intentionally choose, one by one, to close the doors on those noises and to simply be still.

There, in rest and quiet, we don't just find our salvation and strength.[15] We also have a chance of seeing the God who sees us.

Yes, this takes practice. And no, I'm still not very good about it. I'm still prone to flutter, prone to get swallowed up in busyness. I know that B.U.S.Y. means Being Under Satan's Yoke. But the truth is, most of the time, I *like* to move fast. I enjoy having a million things going on, music on the stereo, kids tromping through the house. It's fun to multitask. It's satisfying to check items off a list. It feels good to be in the middle of things.

And you know, I don't think it's *always* bad to be busy.

It's just bad to be *always* busy.

It's unhealthy to get so caught up in the noise that I let it distract me from my wonderful husband sitting there on the bed and waiting to say good morning. And especially from my wonderful God waiting for me to slow down and draw near to Him so that He can draw near to me.[16]

So I'm trying to learn to be still. To consciously seek out times and places where I can breathe deeply and slow down. A time to listen. To seek. To ask and to wait. To rest when I need it.

And in the process, hopefully, to experience the miracle of a perspective change.

choice #8: say thank you

I've long believed that maintaining a thankful attitude is closely tied to seeing God. I've found that making the conscious effort to give thanks "in all circumstances"[17] can be a powerful perspective shifter. Somehow the very act of deliberately verbalizing "thank you," even when we don't feel very thankful, helps us turn our eyes toward God and see more clearly the ways He is blessing us.

I have recently been made even more keenly aware of the potency of a thankful attitude through Ann Voskamp's powerful and poetic book *One Thousand Gifts*. This book is essentially the story of how keeping a gratitude journal—attempting to watch for and write down and give thanks for "one thousand gifts" from God—revolutionized her thinking and her life. She points out that the Greek word used in the New Testament when Jesus gave thanks at the Last Supper was *eucharisteo*, which contains the root words for both "grace" and "joy." And she adds:

> I shape loaves and think how Jesus took the bread and gave thanks ... and then the miracle of the multiplying of the loaves and fishes.
>
> How Jesus took the bread and gave thanks ... and then the miracle of Jesus enduring the cross for the joy set before Him.
>
> How Jesus stood outside Lazarus's tomb, the tears streaming down His face, and He looked up and prayed, "Father, I thank you that you have heard me ..." (John 11:41 NIV). And then the miracle of a dead man rising! Thanksgiving raises the dead! The empty, stiff cadaver surging, the veins full of blood, the alveoli of the lungs filling with oxygen, the coronary arteries full of the whoosh of thrumming life.
>
> How there is thanks ... and then the mind-blowing miracle! I lay loaves in pans and feel years of angst lying down too.

Eucharisteo—thanksgiving—*always precedes the miracle.*[18]

I love that idea, and I've seen it happen in my own life again and again. When I choose to say thank you, something shifts. It may happen immediately, or it may take a little time. But the very act of giving thanks in everything—even the hard things of life—is often the catalyst that makes the miracle of a perspective change happen. Choosing to be grateful, choosing to acknowledge the Author of life and Giver of all good things—including the hard experiences that shape us—keeps us grounded in Truth and seeing rightly. It may be our most powerful key for seeing through the fog.

choice #9: receive the day

My good friend Dr. Bob Grant was the one who first advised me to "receive the day," and I've come to love that phrase. To me it carries such depth of wisdom, and it sums up so beautifully the miraculous shift of perspective that can help us perceive the God who sees us.

It's closely tied with gratitude—opening our hands with thanks to receive what God has for us at any given moment.

It indicates contentment—choosing to be satisfied with what the moment brings, not overanalyzing, not fretting over what we wanted instead.

It indicates a restraint from judgment—or as Jerry puts it, remaining in curiosity and staying out of judgment as to what God is doing. Not imposing my ideas about how God should come to us but welcoming Him into our lives any way He chooses to reveal Himself.

It indicates releasing the illusion of control and relaxing into the reality of God's sovereignty and goodness and grace. Trusting God to give us what we need. Trusting our Father to give us bread, not stones.[19] Trusting that in His hands the universe is "unfolding as it should."[20]

It's a conscious choice, a shift of attitude, a completely different way of thinking. And in my experience, at least, it makes all the difference.

Why not try it?

Receive the day as God gives it—exactly as God gives it. Give thanks. Then open your eyes to the miracle.

Fog or no fog, the mountain is there.

chapter five

blind time

I am still confident of this:
I will see the goodness of the LORD
in the land of the living.

Psalm 27:13

"Hi, Mom. This is Sam. I'm at the airport."

That moment marked one of the most important learning experiences of my life. But to tell it to you right, I need to back up just a little.

Samuel Maltby is my wonderful, beloved, only son. From the moment he arrived from Korea, where he was born, and was placed in my arms, we have shared an amazing bond. He was and is a true treasure of my heart. So I had mixed feelings when, at age ten, he had the opportunity to go away to camp in upstate New York. I was thrilled for him. But oh, it was hard for me to see him go.

All through those weeks Sam was gone, I missed him. And on the morning when he was due to fly back home, I couldn't wait. I was so ready to be with my boy. I'd been thinking about him all week. I'd cleaned his room and put fresh sheets on his bed. I'd gone shopping and bought all his favorite foods. A big, juicy roast was ready for the oven. (My boy loves meat.) I just couldn't wait until it was time to make the drive to Denver to meet his plane.

Then I got a phone call from the camp director. "Your son, Sam, missed his flight this morning," the man said, "so we're going to have to put him on another flight."

"Well, all right." I was disappointed but not too worried. I wrote down the new flight information and went back to getting the house ready for Sam's arrival.

Then, a couple of hours later, just as I about to get in the car for the drive to the airport, the phone rang again: "Mrs. Maltby, we're sorry to tell you, but that other flight your son was supposed to be on was canceled. We're going to have to place him on *another* flight."

At this point, I was starting to get a little concerned, knowing that my ten-year-old was sitting there all by himself at the New York airport. Though I knew the airline was looking out for him, I couldn't help but worry. But what could I do? I wrote down the new flight information again and went back to my work.

But then the phone rang *again*. "We're really sorry, Mrs. Maltby, but the crew on Sam's plane went into overtime and can't fly."

By this time it was about two thirty in the afternoon, and I was getting a little crazy. I was wracking my brain to figure out what to do.

For the next couple of hours I was on the phone and on the Internet, looking at every possible option. I'm a former flight attendant—could I fly him home on a pass or cash in miles and go to meet him? Did I know anyone in New York City who could go to the airport and pick him up? Could I drive my red Suburban all the way from Colorado to New York?

I was talking very loudly to my husband, telling him he needed to be upstairs and as upset about this as I was. And I was thinking constantly about my son. He was the only thing on my mind.

Then, about five thirty that afternoon I got yet another call. This time it was Sam, calling collect. (This was in the days before kids had cell phones.)

"Hi, Mom, this is Sam." His voice was a little plaintive.

I said, "I know!"

He said, "Mom, do you know that I have been at the airport all day long? Haven't you been worried about me?"

"Oh, Samuel," I said, "of course I've been worried. I've been on the Internet. I've been calling everyone I know. I've been doing everything I can to get you home to me. You are the only thing I have been thinking about all day!"

And when I hung up that phone, the Holy Spirit said to me, "Tammy, I do that to you all the time. You are lost in some wilderness place, and you don't think I know. You don't think I see. You do not think I am at work on your behalf. But I am on the *real* World Wide Web. I'm hard at work arranging good things for your life. I've got it all under control, even when you think I've forgotten you."

when we can't see God

That story still helps me a lot when I'm stuck in one of those prolonged times when, no matter how hard I try, I just can't see God.

Those times do happen, you know.

You can do everything right. You can ask God to reveal Himself,
can believe that you will see, can stay alert and look for God in every
corner of your life. You can make the choice, every day, to receive the
day. You can choose, to the best ability, to have eyes to see and ears to
hear and a mind to perceive the God who sees you.

And sometimes it just doesn't work—or it doesn't work the way
you expected.

And there will still be times, sometimes long periods of time,
when you just don't see any evidence that God exists, much less that
He's close to you and working in your life. When everything looks
ordinary or everything looks awful or everything just goes dark.
When you're stuck in some waiting room, wondering if your heavenly Father even knows you're there.

Why can't you see? There are many possible reasons—some you
can control, and some you can't:

- *You're only human.* Living in a flesh-and-blood
  body—complete with hormones, hungers, emotions, and physical/emotional illnesses—by definition clouds our spiritual eyesight.
- *You're too close*—or, more accurately, *God* is
  too close for you to perceive Him. As Leonard
  Sweet puts it, "Jesus can be so close ('closer than a

brother') to us it is like asking a bird to see air or a fish to see water."[1]

- *Your faith is faltering.* "Without faith it is impossible to please God, because anyone who comes to him must believe that he exists and that he rewards those who earnestly seek him."[2]

- *Sin gets in your eyes.* Sin (your own or others') brings with it selfishness, pain, anger, rebellion—all of which can blind us to the presence of God in our lives.

- *You're determined to do it your way.* Rebellion, disobedience, and willfulness all constitute a special variety of sin.

- *It's all about you.* Self-focus may be blocking your ability to see things as they really are. All you can see is how people and events affect you, which is never anything close to the real picture.

- *You're hanging on too tightly.* Your need to control what is happening in your life might keep you from recognizing and accepting something new that God is doing.

- *You're busy and distracted.* It's easy to move so fast and make so much noise that you just can't notice God's quiet coming.

- *Your expectations are too narrow.* Like the people who demanded specific miracles from Jesus, you may be expecting God to show up in a certain

way and refuse to recognize His presence in any
other form.

- *You're forgetting what He's already shown you.*
  You're not taking into account those meaningful
  times in the past when God has been close and
  real to you.

- *You're in denial.* You can't see God because at some
  level you're refusing to recognize a basic dynamic
  in your life (such as an addiction or a problem
  you need to resolve). You can't see God accurately
  because you're closing your eyes to something in
  yourself.

- *Fear skews your vision.* The emotion of fear—or
  stress, anxiety, or depression—can keep you from
  seeing clearly. You may also be a little "resurrection phobic"—nervous about the power of the
  living God in your life.

- *Double-mindedness makes it hard to focus.* Wanting
  more than one conflicting thing (like God and
  money) may be keeping you from focusing clearly
  enough to see Him.

- *Tears blur your sight.* If you're broken emotionally,
  you may have difficulty seeing things clearly, at
  least for a while.

- *You've got a pride problem.* A proud person is
  always looking down on things and people.
  And when you are looking down, it's hard to see
  Someone who is above you.

- *God chooses to remain unseen.* The Bible makes it
  clear that there are times when God hides Himself
  from us, for reasons of His own.

Seeing God, remember, isn't always our choice. It's always God's prerogative to reveal Himself to us or not. And sometimes, He chooses to hide Himself.

When that happens, we're left with a completely different set of choices.

We have to choose how we're going to live when we can't see God.

This, of course, is a big topic. It's something Christians have wrestled with for centuries. There's a ton of literature on so-called "dry seasons" or "dark nights of the soul"—we could just as easily call them "blind times." But I hope I can offer you some encouragement about how you can survive and even thrive during these times.

some possible whys

We can't always know, of course, why God chooses to hide Himself. He's God, and He has His reasons. But I have often found it helpful and even encouraging to spend a little time thinking of the possibilities—some reasons that a loving God *might* choose not to reveal Himself. A look through the Bible suggests plenty of these.

For instance, God might hide Himself in order to protect us. We are mortal creatures living in frail bodies, and there's a limit to how much of God's reality we can handle. Physically seeing God in His fullness would be like looking directly at the sun—our retinas (and most of the rest of us) would be destroyed. Do you remember that scene from *Raiders of the Lost Ark* when the Nazis opened the ark of the covenant? What followed was pure Hollywood, but it made the same point God made to Moses in Exodus 33:20: "You cannot see my face, for no one may look at me and live."

Now, granted, God has ways to get around that, because there are plenty of examples in the Bible where people—even Moses—met with God face-to-face. And we are promised that at some point, when we are freed from these limited bodies, we will all see God that way.[3] But the point still holds. There are many cases when God might choose to hide Himself from us for our own protection. And not just to protect us from being destroyed. I believe He may also protect us from truth we are not (yet) strong enough to handle. God loves us, remember, and is always gentle with us, wooing us rather than overwhelming us. And hiding Himself may sometimes be the best way to do that.

More often, I've come to believe, God hides from us to help us grow and learn. There are some lessons, it seems, that are best learned in the dark.

The story of the Israelites, for example, is clear evidence that overt miracles are no guarantee of faith. To deliver His people from Egypt, God used frogs, blood, illness—you name it. He parted an ocean so they could walk through it. He led them through a wilderness as a very visible pillar of fire and pillar of cloud. He even made food materialize from heaven.

Evidence of His love for them and care for them was constantly in front of their faces. *And yet their faith still faltered.* The minute those visible reminders were removed, they started whining that God had abandoned them. They just couldn't seem to hang on to their faith for very long—and is faith really faith if it's only based on physical evidence?

I think that's often true for us as well: Seeing God is no guarantee of strong faith. In fact, faith often seems to grow stronger in those times when we're waiting for God to show Himself.

The famous eleventh chapter of the book of Hebrews makes that point eloquently, describing person after person who spent almost his or her entire lives waiting to see faith rewarded ... and *died* while still waiting. Yet those people's faith only grew stronger as they continued to wait. That could well be what God has in mind for you during a particular blind time in your life.

Hebrews 11 also hints at yet another reason that God might choose to hide Himself: because He's working on something much bigger than we can understand, much bigger than our individual lives. Writing about all those people who waited a lifetime to see what God would to do, the writer of Hebrews says:

> Not one of these people, even though their lives of faith were exemplary, got their hands on what was promised. God had a better plan for us: that their faith and our faith would come together to make one completed whole, their lives of faith not complete apart from ours.[4]

We all have a hard time understanding that life is not always about us, but it's true. God makes it clear in His Word that though He cares passionately about each of us, though He sees us and watches over us and has big plans for us, His real business is transforming the entire world. He redeems us to be part of a redeemed earth, and He's shaping all of history toward that end. He's working in all dimensions—material, spiritual, temporal—at once. And in the midst of that vast redemptive plan, He often must operate in ways that we just can't see.

seek and find

I believe one of most important reasons God hides Himself from us is that He wants us to seek Him. Not just casually notice Him, but put time and energy and intentionality into finding Him, knowing His ways, understanding His will.

Over and over in the Bible we're urged to do that:

> If from there you seek the LORD your God, you will find him if you look for him with all your heart and with all your soul.[5]

> The LORD searches every heart and understands every motive behind the thoughts. If you seek him, he will be found by you.[6]

> Look to the LORD and his strength; seek his face always.[7]

> I love those who love me, and those who seek me find me.[8]

> You will ... find me when you seek me with all your heart.[9]

> Ask and it will be given to you; seek and you will find; knock and the door will be opened to you.[10]

> God did this so that men would seek him and perhaps reach out for him and find him, though he is not far from each one of us.[11]

Why would God make such a big deal about having us search for Him?

It's certainly not because He's teasing us, keeping out of sight just so we'll have to run around frantically looking for Him. I think it's because He made us and He knows how we work. And it's human nature to seek what we treasure ... and to treasure what we seek.

God wants us to seek Him because He wants us to understand just how important He is to us and because He wants to have a real, living relationship with us.

Have you ever been in one of those friendships where you were always the initiator? Where your friend was always glad to hear from you, but you had to be the one who called? Where your friend was delighted to go out to dinner, but you had to make the plans? How long did that friendship last? You probably eventually lost interest, even if you enjoyed that friend's company. And the friend probably lost interest as well.

I'm not saying God loses interest in us if we're not always seeking Him. But it's certainly difficult to maintain any kind of intimate, real friendship unless both friends put out the effort to be together. And it's hard to value any friendship that doesn't require a little energy and effort.

Notice, by the way, that God says we are to seek His *face,* not His hand. (The Hebrew word for "face" also means "presence."[12]) We often end up looking for God because of what we want Him to give us, to do for us. But what God wants of us is a relationship, not a transaction. He wants us to seek Him for His own sake, to want to be with Him, to desire His presence.

So God calls us to seek Him, even when He's hard to see. Even when He's hidden. He does it because He loves us. And He promises that our seeking will not be in vain. If we throw our hearts into looking for God, we *will* find Him. Or as the psalmist puts it, we will "see the goodness of the LORD in the land of the living."[13]

In the meantime, though, we're left with the question of how we can live in those times when we can't see God. I'd like to suggest a few things that have helped me the most in those times when I found myself wondering if God even knew where I was.

do what you know to do

I have a friend who, after a lifetime of unsuccessfully fighting her weight, managed to lose fifty pounds. When I asked her how she did it, she told me, "I finally figured that I *knew* what to do. I've tried nearly every diet on the planet. I knew what foods are problematic for me. I knew I need smaller portions. I knew I need to exercise every day. I didn't need to be educated. I just needed to do what I knew to do."

That's something I think we need to remember when it comes to those blind times in our lives. We may be waiting to see God, to get more instructions, to be inspired, when what we really need to do is start walking and do what God wants us to do.

And what God wants is no secret. We've got a whole book of instructions. We have the witness of thousands of years of believers and the testimonies of others in His body reminding us to:

- love God with all our hearts and minds and souls and strength.[14]
- love our neighbor as ourselves.[15]
- confess our sins, repent, and accept God's forgiveness. (In my experience, this alone is often enough to give me clearer vision and make it easier for me to see God.)[16]
- forgive as we have been forgiven.[17]
- feed the hungry, clothe the naked, heal the sick, care for orphans and widows, visit prisoners.[18]
- love, support, and encourage our brothers and sisters in the body of Christ.[19]
- trust in God and not lean on our own understanding.[20]

We've got our marching orders. So maybe it's not inappropriate to ask: What are we waiting for? We don't need to have an epiphany to tell us to do those things. We don't need a life-changing vision. We just need to … obey. And interestingly enough, the very act of obedience often helps us see God better.

I love the way Oswald Chambers explains this: "All God's revelations are sealed until they are opened to us by obedience.... God will never reveal more truth about Himself until you have obeyed what you know already."[21]

Sometimes, in fact, I suspect God goes into hiding to nudge us into actually using what He's already given us. He lets us go it alone (or we feel like we're alone) to help us develop confidence and experience in living His way.

I've done that as a parent. When my children were little, I would sometimes let them be outside by themselves or walk to a friend's house without supervision while I'd secretly keep an eye on them. They *needed* that experience of making their way in the world. They needed to learn to function without my constant direction. So I stayed close, but I tried to stay out of their sight, for a little while at least.

I really believe that God does this with us as well. He gives us the freedom to do things on our own because He wants us to grow. It's like He's saying, *You've got a map* (the Bible). *You've got GPS* (the Holy Spirit). *You've got your cell phone* (prayer) *and your instructions* (see above). *You've got My promise that I'll be there if you need Me. So what's stopping you?*

And here's one other wrinkle. In my experience, at least, God often doesn't show Himself *until* I start moving on the path to obedience. It's the very act of doing what I've been told to do that both strengthens my faith and opens my eyes to see more of what God is doing.

I've said it many times, and I believe it with all my heart: You never know what's on the other side of your obedience. With every step, you may well see more of God. Chambers elaborates:

> One reads tomes on the work of the Holy Spirit, when one five minutes of drastic obedience would make things as clear as a sunbeam. "I suppose I shall understand these things some day!" You can understand them now. It is not study that does it, but obedience. The tiniest fragment of obedience, and heaven opens and the profoundest truths of God are yours straight away.[22]

But what if you take a step, or many steps, and nothing seems to change? What if you take step after step, doing what you know to do, and you still feel like you're walking blind?

If that's the case, you might consider something radical. Maybe you don't see because you don't *need* to see.

God is your Father. He knows what you need more than you know it. And that means He knows what you *don't* need. You may be stronger than you think. Your faith may be more robust, your trust more solid than you realize. You may have the precious ability to walk in faith, not sight.

But you'll never know that, either, until you take a step.

tell yourself your stories

As I have mentioned, God once told Moses, "No one may see me and live."[23] He said that because Moses had requested, "Show me your glory."[24] And though the answer was a protective "No," God did offer a workaround. What He did was tuck Moses into a little crevice of rock. Then He passed by in His full glory, but He covered Moses' face with His hand. Only when He was moving away did He take His hand away, letting Moses catch only a glimpse of His back.

That story has always amused me a little—that image of Moses peeking out from the rock to catch a rearview glimpse of the Deity. But I also think that story hints at an important truth that can help us make it through those blind times of our lives.

The truth is, a lot of our views of God are rearview glimpses. Sometimes we see Him best by looking back at our lives. And when we just can't see God in our present, quite often we can bolster our faith and find encouragement by choosing to look back.

Philip Yancey tells us,

> The life of faith consists of living in the past and in the future. I live in the past in order to ground myself in what God has already done, as a way of gaining confidence in what he might do again. Relating to an invisible God involves certain handicaps: with no sensory evidence in the present, we must look backward to remind ourselves of who it is we are relating to.[25]

Large sections of the Bible reflect this truth that we often see God best in retrospect. Story after biblical story illustrates how God has acted and how God's people have experienced Him. These are stories the Hebrews told one another over the centuries, as a way of remembering. (They had to do this because they were *always* forgetting!) They are stories the disciples and the early Christians told themselves. And they're stories that inform us of God's faithfulness through the ages. The more often we read them, the better picture we get of who God is, what He has done in the world, and what He may be doing at any given moment.

But rearview stories about God don't just have to come from the Bible. I find that when I take the time to look back at my life, to tell my own stories to myself, my vision sharpens and my faith is increased. These stories of how God has moved in my own life give me strength to keep on going even when I don't have a clue what God's doing *now*.

Here's just one example, one that's very near to my heart.

I had a speaking engagement a couple of years back in Grand Junction, Colorado. I was to speak there for several nights, and the sponsoring church had arranged lodging for my husband, Jerry, and me. But only eighty women signed up for the weekend—a much smaller turnout than I expected.

I hate to admit this, but by the time that weekend rolled around, I was in a very grumpy mood about the whole thing. In fact, I almost called to cancel. But duty finally won out. I asked God to change my attitude, then got into the car for the trip there.

I didn't feel any better when we got to town and found ourselves driving through a shabby part of town, looking for the place where we were supposed to spend the night. I realized the church must have arranged to put us in a bed-and-breakfast instead of a hotel, and from the looks of the houses we drove by, I wasn't expecting much.

We drove down the road, counting off numbers, looking for what I was sure would be a rundown little B and B. Then, to my surprise, the landscape seemed to open up. To our left was a lovely view of grapevines backing up to mountains. I thought, *Wow. Grapevines in Colorado—how charming is that?*

We drove on, still looking at numbers. Then I spotted the sign: "238 Two Rivers Vineyard." We looked down the long driveway and spotted a Swiss-style chalet nestled among those grapevines.

We were a little confused. The sign said nothing about a B and B. But we drove down the driveway, and a woman stepped out of the chalet to meet us.

"Is this where we're supposed to be?" I asked. "Is it really a vineyard?"

The hostess answered, "Yes. Welcome, Ms. Maltby. We are so glad you are here. There is a basket of goodies in your room—some local chocolates, an assortment of fruit and cheeses, and some other things. Have a wonderful visit."

She showed us to a luxurious corner suite. And there in a beautiful silver wine chiller was a bottle of the Two Rivers chardonnay. "It's our best-selling wine," the hostess told me. "I think you will love it."

All I could do was stand there with my mouth open. Because that chardonnay was the very same kind Jerry had opened the night he first mentioned marriage to me. "I'm not going to date you," he said back then. "I'm not even going to court you. But I am going to court your children, and when they fall in love with me, I know you will too." Then he pulled out the bottle of Two Rivers. "I want to toast to the day that two rivers become one. My intention this next year is to make you my wife."

You can see why I was so amazed as I stood in that beautiful room in that breathtaking vineyard, looking at that significant bottle of wine. It was as if God was standing there smiling, saying, *I just knew you would love this. I couldn't wait to show it to you. Now, aren't you glad you came?*

That was the beginning of a memorable weekend—a fruitful conference, a lovely and hospitable host, and a wonderful time for Jerry and me together. And I like to tell myself that story often to remind me of God's faithfulness in big and little things, His thoughtfulness, His amazing love. Every time I remember, my ability to trust Him grows a little more.

The Israelites used to pile up pillars of stones—stones of remembrance—to commemorate times when God moved powerfully and showed Himself to them. Jerry and I keep an empty Two Rivers bottle in our house for the same reason—as a reminder of that weekend when God showed us so tenderly that He really does see us.

I've come to believe that remembrance is one of the keys to contentment as a Christian—especially in the blind times of our lives. It's important to remind ourselves of all those times when God has been faithful, to rehearse them in our minds, to write them down and tell our children and our children's children. When we do that, we not only provide a testimony to others—we provide it for ourselves. With story after story of what we've seen of God, we can walk ourselves through the times when seeing is more difficult.

don't try to walk alone

"Where two or three come together in my name," Jesus said emphatically, "there am I with them."[26] In other words, if you want to see

God, you should hang out with His people. Ohio pastor Robert A. Arbogast expresses this wonderfully:

> What's the visible part of any person? The body! In this case, the body of Christ....
>
> Do you want to see Jesus? Look around you! In this room, look to your left, to your right, look in front of you, behind you. Scripture says *we* are the body of Christ. *We* make Christ visible.
>
> For some reason, I think of this most often at Wednesday prayers—probably because we're small in number—but Jesus promised to be where two or three gather in his name. So I sit at Wednesday prayers and smile, picturing Jesus there among us, next to us, in front of us. But that's not quite right. Jesus *is* there. But he's there in the person sitting to my right or to my left; he's there in person in front of me or behind me. Seeing them, I see Jesus with me, with us.
>
> Now I don't for a moment imagine that I'm seeing Jesus this way in all his perfection and glory. No doubt seeing Jesus here, in each other, we see through a glass darkly. Nevertheless, somehow, by God's grace and according to the Word of Christ, this *is* the body of Christ, *this* is God, somehow, made visible.[27]

I can't tell you how often I have found this to be true—not only within the walls of church buildings, but also and maybe especially around the dinner table, at weddings and funerals, over cups of coffee and tea. I believe this is intentional on God's part. He wants us to encourage and challenge one another in our walks of faith. To support one another. To love one another. To help one another through difficult times—and especially through those times when we *can't* see God.

I stress this because there's a tendency, when we're going through a blind time, to pull away from other believers. We may be embarrassed. We may be confused or have conflicted feelings about God. We may be worried about our testimony or what others will think of what we're going through.

But that's exactly why we need our brothers and sisters so much when we're having trouble seeing. We need their prayers. We need their insights. We need their hugs and reassurance, their partnership in service, their stories about their own blind times and God's faithfulness. We need their reminders that God really does see us. (And of course, they need this from us as well.)

There are certainly times when we need to seek solitude, to quiet our hearts in order to sharpen our vision. But even these quiet times will go better if we've asked for prayers and told someone of our struggle. We were never meant to walk through life alone. Especially not when we're walking in the dark.

surrender the orphan spirit

As I have mentioned, adoption is something that is very close to my heart. Not only were two of my children adopted internationally, but eleven of my nieces and nephews came to us through adoption. I love the way my very Midwestern, very Scandinavian extended family has grown into a multicolored, multinational one that, to me, looks a lot like the family of God.

Adoption is also close to my heart because I, too, am an adopted child. When I accepted Christ, I was officially received into God's family—an adopted daughter of the King, and one with full rights as His daughter.

Romans 8:15 expresses this eloquently: "For you did not receive the spirit of bondage again to fear, but you received the Spirit of adoption by whom we cry out, 'Abba, Father.'"[28] But even before Paul penned those words, Jesus gave the disciples this promise of spiritual adoption: "I will talk to the Father, and he'll provide you another Friend so that you will always have someone with you.... *I will not leave you orphaned.*"[29]

To me the promise is clear. When we receive the Holy Spirit, we become fully fledged members of God's family. Not stepchildren. Not foster kids. Definitely not orphans. God is our real Father. We are His real daughters and sons. Christ is our real Brother. We are such a close-knit family that we actually become part of one another.

But what if the adopted child has trouble *feeling* like part of the family? That happens with the earthly adoptions of kids who went through significant trauma or neglect before their adoptions. Those kids may have trouble connecting with others, trusting, believing they are truly loved. Even after they're adopted, they may struggle with what I call an orphan spirit.

But the orphan spirit doesn't just afflict legally adopted kids. Anyone who has been hurt deeply at some point in her life can find herself marked in this way. If you've felt abandoned or rejected, suffered trauma, or felt betrayed by someone you love—especially when you were young—you may be carrying it too.

Deep down, you expect to be abandoned, rejected, betrayed, or traumatized again. So you live your life both on the offensive and the defensive—running from relationships, lashing out to protect yourself, latching on to anyone you think may offer you comfort, or trying too hard to prove yourself, to show the world you are worthy of your place in it. And yet none of these protective measures is sufficient to make you feel truly loved and cared for. No one can love you enough. No one can give you enough. Your pain has left you with the deep-down certainty that no matter what happens, you will always be alone, unprotected, unloved.

This doesn't mean you walk around as a quivering, nervous wreck. Your orphan spirit may be deeply buried or disguised, and it may lie dormant as long as things are going well. But when things go wrong, especially in relationships, that's when the orphan spirit swoops in to take over, making you angry, defensive, needy … and partially blind.

Yes, blind.

Because that's the thing about the orphan spirit. Once it takes over, you may find it almost impossible to see anything except through its filter—including your relationship with God. This makes the issue of seeing God problematic and those times when God hides Himself especially painful. Because an orphan spirit can survive a spiritual adoption as well as a legal one. That defensive, needy orientation can easily become a stronghold in our lives.

We may rejoice in the fact that we have been adopted by the Father and find great joy in His presence. But when the fog rolls in and we can't perceive God's presence, the orphan spirit kicks in, and we panic. We just know we're being abandoned *again*. We're sure we're being punished or rejected—left as orphans—even though Jesus promised specifically that He wouldn't do that.

If you're feeling especially alone, abandoned, frightened, and panicked, you might want to consider whether an orphan spirit is rearing its head. You'll be able to walk in the darkness a lot more easily if you can manage, with God's help, to surrender that spirit. It will take some time. Like forgiveness, surrendering an orphan spirit is something you'll probably have to do again and again. Life events can reveal one layer after another. It is a process—usually a lifelong one. But simply recognizing that an orphan spirit may be coloring your perceptions can help you walk through those blind times in your life with a little less panic. It can help you begin to replace your defensiveness with trust. You may even come to see that this blind time in your life is part of God's loving strategy to help you live into your spiritual adoption with true confidence—letting the reality that you are a loved member of God's family take hold of you in a deeper way than ever before.

worship while you wait

Have you ever had to wait for a check to arrive before you had the money to pay an important bill or do something you deeply desired to do?

Like many Americans, my husband and I were hit hard by the recession of 2009. For Jerry, who has worked many years in real estate and investing, the hit was devastating. Some of his investments evaporated overnight. Some of his projects fizzled. A big portion of what he had could not be accessed or liquidated.

The downturn in publishing hit me about the same time. A contract was canceled. Expected royalties didn't materialize. Speaking gigs were languishing, and a part-time business venture brought in no revenue.

I don't want to whine too much here. I know that even in our reduced state, we were privileged compared to most of the world. We didn't go hungry. We had what we needed. And God did provide for us, sometimes in quite amazing ways. But for Jerry especially, it was a scary and humbling thing to repeatedly be put in that position of waiting for a check, not knowing when it would come and what it would contain.

But in the midst of that very difficult time, Jerry shared a concept that has come to mean the world to me. It happened during one of those times when we were short on funds for an important obligation and had no idea whether those funds would materialize in time.

We prayed, of course. Then I said to Jerry, "What do we do now?"

He answered, "We worship while we wait."

Don't you just love that? To me, it encapsulates so much of the life we do here on earth while we're waiting for God to show Himself. It summarizes the attitude that can get us through, the choice that can keep us going day after day when the fog surrounds us and we can't see our hands in front of our faces.

Maybe we can't see what's going to happen next. But while we're waiting to find out, we can choose to believe that God sees us. We can praise Him. We can thank Him for what He's done in our lives and what (whatever!) He's going to do.

We can choose to worship while we wait.

The Message translation of Romans 5:3–5 eloquently describes the difference this choice can make:

> We continue to shout our praise even when we're hemmed in with troubles, because we know how troubles can develop *passionate patience* in us, and how that patience in turn forges the tempered steel of virtue, keeping us alert for whatever God will do next. In alert expectancy such as this, we're never left feeling shortchanged. Quite the contrary—we can't round up enough containers to hold everything God generously pours into our lives through the Holy Spirit!

Look carefully at that phrase *passionate patience.* In other translations, this is usually translated as "perseverance." But to me that's such a joyless, heads-down, nose-to-the-grindstone word, and it doesn't speak as powerfully to those times when we're just doing what we can, waiting for God to show up.

Passionate patience—that's what makes it possible to worship while you wait. It's what sustained all those folks in Hebrews 11 as they lived out their lives, waiting for God's promises to be fulfilled. It's what kept Jerry and me sane and grounded (well, sort of sane and grounded) during that very scary time. It's what makes it possible to sing in the dark or survive our time in the waiting room.

It's waiting without being resigned or losing hope.

It's choosing to expect a miracle even when all odds seem against it, but also choosing to accept *whatever* God brings—because whatever God brings into our lives is good, and whatever comes into our lives, period, can be used for good.

It's choosing to praise God even when you can't see Him. To stay excited about His possibilities even when you're unsure what will happen or when.

It's not just plodding, grit-your-teeth waiting. (Though, to be honest, sometimes it feels that way.) Instead, it's moving along with your head up—moving in expectation, because you really expect that something's going to happen. Because you know that whether you can see it or not, the God of the universe is at work in your life and in the world. He will keep His promises. He will show up when the time is right—when His time is right.

And yes, passionate patience is a choice. Sometimes it's a hard choice, though it's based on very good evidence. But in those times when everything seems dark and we don't have a clue where God is or what He's doing, passionate patience can keep us going.

the promise that makes it all possible

There will probably be times in your life—many times—when you don't see God. You may even feel that He's a million miles away, that He's forgotten all about you. But He's moving heaven and earth to work things out for good and bring you home. You can trust Him to give you whatever you need to become who He intends for you to be: His grown-up, perfect, beloved daughter or son.

Whatever you need—I believe that's God's bottom line when it comes to revealing Himself.

Do you remember the story of Jesus' disciple Thomas, who struggled with believing that his Lord was really risen from the dead? "Doubting Thomas" is often dismissed as sort of a failure, but to me his story is a beautiful example of how God will give us what we need.

It wasn't that Thomas didn't want to believe. He just couldn't. The past weeks had been too stressful, too traumatic. Everything Thomas thought he knew had been overturned, and he just didn't have what it took to believe what his fellow disciples were telling him. Thomas *needed* concrete evidence that Jesus was alive. And Jesus gave him what he needed:

> Jesus came and stood among them and said, "Peace be with you!" Then he said to Thomas, "Put your finger here; see my hands. Reach out your hand and put it into my side. Stop doubting and believe."
>
> Thomas said to him, "My Lord and my God!"
>
> Then Jesus told him, "Because you have seen me, you have believed; blessed are those who have not seen and yet have believed."[30]

Was Jesus chiding Thomas when He said, "Blessed are those who have not seen and have yet believed"? I don't think so.

Blessed in the New Testament doesn't necessarily mean "better" or "approved." It means "happy" or "peaceful." I think Jesus was saying, "My friend, it would be so much easier on you if you could believe without having to see everything with your own eyes. You'll enjoy more peace if you develop more faith. But never mind. What you need, I'll give you. Look at Me. Touch Me. Believe in Me. I'm here." [31]

I find that tremendously reassuring. We can trust God to give us what we need and to show Himself accordingly. If you need to see Him, He will show Himself to you … and take your breath away. If it's better for Him to be hidden, He will hide but still stay close.

If you really need reassurance and affirmation, you can cry out, and He'll be there—in the Spirit and also, often, through someone in His body whom you can see and hear and touch and smell. If you need to grow some confidence and faith, He'll let you step out on your own, bolstered by your memories of those times He's shown Himself to you.

You *will* see the goodness of God in the land of the living. It may sometimes be just a glimpse of glory, a murky view in a mirror, or a revelation that sticks in your memory. But it will be enough.

And someday, when your life is through, you and the Lord of the universe will behold each other as He's intended all along.

Face-to-face.

chapter six

when bad things happen

> The minute I said, "I'm slipping, I'm falling,"
> your love, God, took hold and held me fast.
> When I was upset and beside myself,
> you calmed me down and cheered me up....
> GOD became my hideout,
> God was my high mountain retreat.
>
> Psalm 94:18–19, 22 MSG

The phone call came while I was just about to embark on writing this chapter. It concerned my friend Mona—my beautiful colleague and helper who has had my back for endless gatherings—and her firstborn son, Mitchell. Only twenty-three and newly embarked on a career as an electrician, Mitchell was a good-looking, fun-loving young man with a bright future in front of him. But there had been an accident. Suddenly, in a squeal of tires and the crunch of a motorcycle helmet, Mitchell was gone, killed on impact. And Mona, a woman of profound faith, was devastated.

I'll never forget my friend's frantic sobs as we gathered around her, desperate to find a way to help. "How will we survive?" she kept asking. "How will we ever get through this? It's like someone took a knife and carved a canyon in my heart. I can't breathe. Maybe I don't even want to."

I know so many people—good Christians who loved God and trusted Him—who have found themselves transported against their wills to the place where Mona was traveling now, a place you could call Traumaland. These people have experienced one or more of those out-of-sequence, out-of-order watershed moments that turn all of life upside down. They wake up one morning and find themselves living in what seems like a foreign country, where everything looks completely different and they feel utterly lost.

It may have happened to you, too—that phone call or discovery that tilted your world on its axis. At this moment you may be living through your own personal or family trauma. Or you may hear of disaster on the news and realize, with a catch in your throat, that it could happen to you, too.

Trouble may hit with tornado force and then move on, leaving you to blink in the sunshine at the ruin of your "normal" life. It may creep in slowly, insidiously, like a fog or a drought, gradually obscuring the landscape and leaving nothing but exhaustion in its wake. Or a seemingly insignificant incident could unfold into one devastating revelation after another.

The troubles that can afflict us are as familiar as the daily headlines:

- an unexpected or sudden bereavement.
- a personal attack on one or more family members … such as a rape, mugging, or home invasion.
- a legal crisis or imprisonment.
- a shocking revelation … sexual abuse, a gay life-style, mounting debt … or a series of revelations.
- a divorce.
- a frightening medical diagnosis.
- the loss of a job or ministry position.
- a sniper or school shooting.
- a natural disaster like a tornado or hurricane.
- a car or bus or airline crash.
- a mental or emotional breakdown.
- the loss of a home through fire, flood, or fore-closure.
- the birth of a child with a severe disability.
- an addiction in the family … drugs, alcohol, gam-bling, shopping.
- infertility, miscarriage, or stillbirth.
- an elderly parent's decline.
- fill in your own trauma here … or your deepest fear.

Any of these experiences is quite sufficient to turn your life upside down. And most of them bring other problems with them as well. A death (even an expected one) brings shock, grief, confusion ... then the difficulties of rearranging life to cope with loss. A divorce brings legal issues, worries about children, grief and anger, perhaps a drastic change in standard of living. A chronic illness involves financial strain, fear and worry, the logistics of hospitalization. A house fire or flood may bring cascading experiences of loss as the extent of the damage becomes known—not to mention issues of insurance, living space, rebuilding.

Trauma, in other words, changes the very fabric of normal.

It also changes the entire dynamic of seeing and being seen by God.

You have to face the question of where God is when bad things happen. More specifically, it's the question of what He's doing—or not doing—to make things better.

That's not a new question, of course. Book after book and sermon after sermon have been written about the so-called "problem of evil." I've heard quite a few in my day—attempts to explain how evil can persist in the presence of an all-loving, all-knowing, all-powerful God. In my experience, these discussions tend to fall into two types.

One is an argument, a theological speculation, an exploration of ideas.

The other is a cry of need.

And while hashing out ideas can be helpful—or unavoidable— it's the cry of need that matters most to me in my life and the lives of those I care about.[1]

Sometimes it does come in the form of *why*: "Why has this happened?"

Just as often, in my experience, it's a plaintive cry of *how?*: "How will I ever survive? How will I make it through my doubts? How can I move forward? Will life ever be normal again?"

There's a *when* element, such as in Mona's question: "When will my life feel normal again?"

And in the midst of it all is that cry of *Who?*: "Who is this God that has asked me to trust Him, who promises to be with me and care for me and redeem and restore me? Now that all this has happened, how can I trust Him? Where is He, anyway? And why isn't He doing anything to help me? Is God even there?"

when trauma touches faith

I met a gentleman with those kinds of questions in an unusual place—the first-class section of an airplane. And I almost didn't meet him at all.[2]

I was on my way home from a speaking engagement, and I was scheduled to lead a Beth Moore Bible study that very evening. The problem was, I hadn't done my homework. If you've ever done a Beth Moore study, you know it requires you to actually dig into the Word. Just the week before, I had admonished the women in my group about doing their homework. I couldn't face them without having mine done.

The good news was that I had a two-and-a-half-hour plane ride, and I had been upgraded to first class. If I could just focus without interruption, I could get all my study done on the plane and be ready for that night's meeting. When a well-dressed, important-looking gentleman settled into the seat next to me, I thought, *Oh, good. Businessmen* never *want to talk on a flight!* And that was a sure sign to me I wouldn't be interrupted.

I was making good progress when the attendant asked our food preferences. And my growling stomach told me I definitely needed a meal. As we ate, the gentleman made a little joke about the plastic knives and forks. He had a noticeable British accent.

I barely nodded at him. I didn't want to engage.

After dinner, we both went back to work. But the ice had been broken. My seatmate glanced over at my open Bible. "Are you a Christian?" And my immediate response was, *Oh no. He's a Christian too, and he's going to want to talk about spiritual things. And I just don't have time....*

I just glanced at him and said, "Yes, I am."

"Really?" he said. "I'm an agnostic."

I thought, *Are you kidding me?* Oh, brother, there was no way I was getting out of this conversation. After all, isn't that the whole purpose of Bible study, to learn how to react in situations like this? So I shut my book, and we struck up a conversation.

I quickly found out that I was talking to a brilliant and wealthy man—a biologist by background, the head of a prestigious research foundation. And he wanted to talk about faith. I kept thinking, *Really, God? Me talking faith with a brilliant agnostic scientist? You have quite a sense of humor!*

We started talking about angels and creation and why I believe that God really cares about who we are. He told me he was a lapsed Catholic. And at some point in the conversation, I sensed the Holy Spirit saying to me, *Take him back to the time*

when he was a young boy and ask him when he stopped believing that
God saw him.

So I asked him that question. And he started telling me a story about being twelve years old, his mother dying, and a priest trying to comfort him by saying, "God is taking your mother because He needs her more than you do."

The story stopped there. My seatmate couldn't go any further because he had started to shake and sob uncontrollably. He couldn't speak. Neither could I. I thought, *Oh, my goodness. This man is going to have a heart attack or a nervous breakdown right here in first class!*

Finally he excused himself and went to the restroom. I just sat there, stunned, until he returned to his seat and apologized for losing control. He also said, "That's the first time I've cried in twenty-eight years. It's just that ... thinking about what that priest said ..."

I nodded. "You believed God betrayed you. You believed God took your mother." We talked a little more, and he began to weep again. Again he had to retreat to the bathroom. He had kept everything under wraps for so long, but now it was breaking through. He was reliving the moment that changed everything—when the bottom was falling out of his life and someone told him God was the reason for his pain.

He was gone for a long time, and while he was gone I wondered about how that moment of trauma had touched that boy. You see, I'm convinced that it's not the trauma itself that does the most damage in our lives. It's the false conclusions we draw about God that leave the biggest scars. It's the mistaken belief that God doesn't care or isn't in control or that He actually sets out to hurt us. And believing such a thing is just too painful. It feels safer to believe that God doesn't see us—or that He doesn't even exist.

My new friend finally returned to his seat, his handsome face bearing evidence of his emotional breakdown. I didn't quite know what to say, but I had to say something. So I just blurted, "It's not true. What that priest told you was a lie." The priest had probably been grasping clumsily for something to say to a hurting boy. Unfortunately, his words had just added to the injury and confusion.

"God saw you then," I said softly, "and He sees you now. He would never have taken a boy's mother away just because He 'needed her in heaven.'"

From there our conversation became wide-ranging. He wanted to know what the Bible had to say about the problem of evil. What about free will? Why do the innocent suffer? I showed him places in my Bible I had marked—Scriptures about God and His persistent love for us and about Jesus, who understood our pain and died for us. We talked for the duration of that two-and-a-half-hour flight, with me flipping through the Bible and my new friend weeping intermittently.

As we were landing, I said, "I never really introduced myself. My name's Tammy."

He said his name was Jonathan, and he handed me his business card. As we waited for the signal to deplane, I remembered he'd mentioned he was married. "Is your wife agnostic as well?" I asked.

"No," he said. "She's a faith person. She doesn't go to church, but she goes to something called a Bible study. In fact, I recognized the author's name on that book you're reading because my wife goes to the same kind of study."

I laughed out loud when I heard that. If that man's wife went to a Beth Moore study, surely that group of women had been praying for just such an encounter in his life. And maybe there was a way I could take it just a step further. "You know, there's a book I think you'd enjoy. It was written by a very intelligent man, an Oxford professor, who was an atheist but ended up becoming a Christian. If I send you one of his books, would you read it?"

"If you send it to me," he said, "I'll read it."

After I got home—well, after I led the Bible study and had to confess I hadn't done the homework—I dug up a copy of C. S. Lewis's *Mere Christianity* and sent it to the address on Jonathan's business card. He emailed me that he had found it to be a very "profound read." We emailed back and forth a few times, then lost track of each other. But that remarkable encounter has stuck in my mind over the years.

It's a beautiful example of the way the God who sees us orchestrates unexpected and healing encounters. God saw me, put me next to Jonathan so he could see the Beth Moore book, and nudged me to see the pain beneath a very polished and prosperous exterior. And that encounter became a catalyst for Jonathan to see that his little-boy assumptions about God might need to be reconsidered. I've prayed many times that somehow, out of that encounter, he was able to finally see the God who saw him.

But more to the point, this story shows how trauma can affect our view of God—and how a misconception about God can rob us of the comfort and help we need during hard times. I want to weep when I think how that priest's misguided statements about God kept a boy from turning to God when he needed Him so desperately.

That can happen so easily, especially in times of trial. Even those of us who know God can jump to wrong conclusions about His character and intentions for us. If we let that happen, we can miss what He's doing in our lives.

a vision for trauma's aftermath

Since you've gotten this far in this book, you know I believe with my whole heart that God always sees us, always loves us, and is actively and redemptively involved in our lives at any given point, even when terrible, awful things have turned our lives upside down. No, God doesn't typically intervene directly and remove the struggles in our lives. No, He doesn't always act in ways we can understand. That's where all those discussions about humanity's free will and God's sovereignty come in.

I absolutely believe, however, that what we've learned about God remains true even when life turns upside down. No matter what the trauma, He can be trusted to bring comfort in the short term and restoration in the long run—plus His presence in the midst of our pain.

I've also seen too much pain to insist that any of this comes easily. Trauma is real and damaging. God's mercy can be severe. And sometimes the truth only becomes true as you live through it … or as you see it in someone else's eyes.

Which brings us back to the *how* question.

How do you get past those times of trauma, those times of need? How do you trust God when it feels like He's let you down?

How do you even want to?

When you've been hurt, when you're confused, when the worst is supposed to be over but the problems stick like cockleburs, hope can be the last thing you want. Sometimes it hurts too much to hope—especially when you suspect your life will never be the same again. Sometimes "God sees you" can feel like a bitter reality instead of an encouraging one.

So is there a way to move forward? Is it worth the effort to rebuild your life?

That's exactly the dilemma the nation of Judah faced many thousands of years ago. They brought a lot of their trouble on themselves—by ignoring the prophets, by worshipping false gods, by breaking their covenant with Yahweh. But still, the events that rocked their world were shocking and painful.

First, their land was invaded by foreigners. Their best and brightest young people were carted away to serve the king of Babylon. Then the whole nation—men, women, and children—was taken into captivity. People were forced from their homes and into exile. The beautiful temple was burned to the ground.

Before they knew what was happening, God's people found themselves, quite literally, in a foreign land. They established homes and raised children. They found ways to make a living. But they were still exiles, still far from home, still suffering the trauma of displacement. They were probably wondering whether it was a good thing that God had seen them. Whether He saw their present need or whether there was anything worthwhile in their future.

Then came good news. The Persian king Cyrus, who had conquered Babylon, agreed to let the Jews go home and rebuild their temple. More than forty-two thousand Jews followed a governor named Zerubbabel and the high priest Joshua back to Jerusalem to begin getting their lives back. They even laid the foundations for rebuilding the temple. But then the work stalled. Some lost interest when they realized the new temple wouldn't be as beautiful as the first one. Some were preoccupied with personal projects. Drought hit the land, harvests were poor, and the people who had occupied the country in the Jews' absence kept stirring up trouble. Progress on the temple ground to a halt. No work was done on the temple for eighteen years, and no one even seemed to care.[3]

But once again, God cared. He wanted to restore His people more than they even wanted to be restored … and more than they believed was possible.

He sent two prophets—Haggai and Zechariah—to Zerubbabel with very specific messages for him and his priest-partner Joshua. They were messages of hope, and I think they may resonate with anyone asking *why* questions and *how* questions of the God who sees us.

First, God assured Zerubbabel through the visions of Zechariah that there would be restoration and that life would be good again for God's people. The temple would be built. Safety and prosperity would return:

> Once again men and women of ripe old age will sit
> in the streets of Jerusalem, each with cane in hand
> because of his age. The city streets will be filled with
> boys and girls playing there.…
>
> The seed will grow well, the vine will yield its
> fruit, the ground will produce its crops, and the

heavens will drop their dew. I will give all these things
as an inheritance to the remnant of this people.[4]

Second, God made it clear that He was the one who would do all
the heavy lifting in this restoration. He saw His people and had not
forgotten them. (The name *Zechariah* actually means "God remembers"![5]) He was going to make it happen, and restoration would be
His gift: "'Not by might nor by power, but by my Spirit,' says the
LORD Almighty."[6]

At the same time, there were things Zerubbabel and Joshua and
all the people had to do. They needed to pull together and do what
they could, even if their contribution seemed too small and the possible outcomes not worth the effort. Speaking of the temple, God
said:

> Who of you is left who saw this house in its former
> glory? How does it look to you now? Does it not
> seem to you like nothing? But now be strong, O
> Zerubbabel.... Be strong, O Joshua.... Be strong,
> all you people of the land ... and *work*. For I am
> with you....[7]

> *Who despises the day of small things?* Men will
> rejoice when they see the plumb line in the hand
> of Zerubbabel.[8]

Finally, God made it clear that there was a purpose for all this
restoration. It wasn't just to make God's people happy again, but to

make His people a blessing to others: "As you have been an object of cursing among the nations, O Judah and Israel, so will I save you, and you will be a blessing."⁹

Haggai and Zechariah were sent to Zerubbabel and Joshua for a single purpose—to stir up their hope after trauma and get them moving again toward new, better lives. God wanted to assure them that He saw them and that good things lay ahead. I think that's a word we need when trauma has been part of our lives. It's the place to start—the word from the Lord that makes moving forward possible. From there, we can take it a little further.

No one person can give another a foolproof guide for surviving painful experiences. People are just too different—and the God who sees each of us individually deals with us in different ways. But here are just a few of the keys I've discovered that seem to make a big difference in making it through a traumatic time.¹⁰

lean! lean! lean!

First, you likely won't make it through your time of difficulty without help—maybe a lot of help. The good news is that help will be available. The bad news: It's not always easy to accept the help that's available.

Pride can be your biggest enemy here. Sometimes we don't want to admit we need help. Some of us are used to being the ones who give to others, and receiving can feel downright humiliating.

My friend Liza Kendall Christian, who lost her Oregon home to a wildfire started by a vagrant with a cigarette, tells me that this was a significant challenge for her. In fifteen minutes, she went from being an established homeowner with a home business to not even having a toothbrush or a change of underwear. She tells me that being forced to depend on other people for every necessity taught her profound lessons in compassion, humility, mercy, trust, patience, and gratitude—lessons that still resonate in her life today.[11]

Liza also learned that help doesn't necessarily arrive in the form we expected—or wanted. Many people who go through trauma discover, in fact, that their greatest help comes from unexpected sources. People you barely know may turn out to play a significant role in your recovery and restoration. People you counted on may disappoint you. You may not see the signs you envisioned would reveal God's presence and direction.

When this has happened to me, I've found it helpful to remind myself that all my help, ultimately, is from the Lord—but He sends it through all kinds of messengers. At various times in my long journey, I have found much help in the words of Scripture and the still, small voice of the Holy Spirit. I have also been helped by pastors and spiritual advisers, by my extended family, by support groups, by churches I was a part of, by loving Christians outside my particular community, by professional counselors—Christian and secular—as well as by medical doctors, lawyers, people who sat next to me on planes, and authors who wrote life-changing books.

Should I listen equally to all these voices? I don't think so. I have a responsibility to test the voices against Scripture and the Holy Spirit, to seek sound counsel, to be as discerning and wise as I possibly can. At the same time, I don't have a right to reject God's help just because it comes in a form that hurts my pride or causes me discomfort.

I would go one step further here, because it's not just a matter of whether we accept help that's offered. I believe we also have a responsibility, to whatever extent we can manage, to actively *seek* help for ourselves and those we love. In cases of severe depression, post-traumatic stress disorder, and other extreme responses to trauma, professional therapy of some kind will almost certainly be needed.

Such help can be an invaluable gift from God, but only if we're willing to accept it. And often it's hard to accept God's way of providing for us until we're willing to let go of our expectations.

let it go

Letting go essentially means giving up on getting your own way in life—loosening your grip on the way you thought it was supposed to be. If you insist on dictating the terms of your comfort and your restoration, you may be missing how God comes to you in unexpected forms.

Letting go also means accepting the reality that you don't really "get over" a severe loss. Your life really won't be the same. What you have lost through your hard times really can't be replaced—not if it was truly important to you. But you can be *restored*. Life can be good again, even if it won't be the same.

William Ritter, a Methodist minister whose grown son committed suicide, expresses this reality poignantly:

Some people go through a crisis and say, "I've got to get back to my old self." But that's a fruitless quest. You will never get back to your "old self." For the crisis has taken your "old self" with it. You can never get it back. Ever. But that doesn't mean you can't come out with something. For one of the strangest, yet most sublime, facts of human existence is that something beneficial can often be harvested from life's most devastating experiences.[12]

give yourself time to heal (but don't stay in camp too long)

My sister Twyla brought this truth vividly home to me when she compared the experience of trauma to living in a war zone. In war, everything you do is focused on survival. You are constantly in crisis, constantly running on adrenaline, slogging through rice paddies or deserts with your meager belongings in little carts or on your back, dodging bullets, crawling on your belly, doing whatever you must to survive.

Then comes the time when you've finally escaped the war zone, and you find yourself in a refugee camp. You're not home; you're not in your final destination; your problems are far from resolved. But at least you have a place to lay down your burdens for a little while. The primary trauma is over.

When you reach that point, you face both great grace and great danger. This place of respite is just what you need to begin to heal.

You can breathe a little easier. You can smile again (sometimes) and organize your thoughts.

When you reach that point—when the all-consuming tasks of dealing with trauma are behind you, even for a while—it's important to take the time to rest. You need the chance to breathe. And God will provide you that time. That's the grace.

But what's the danger?

The danger is that you could get too comfortable in camp and miss out on God's full restoration.

Once you find a little bit of safety, a little bit of comfort, a little taste of normal, you can find yourself hesitant to risk anymore. So you stay in the refugee camp and refuse to budge. You become like the Jews who stayed in Babylon instead of returning to Jerusalem or the leaders who became distracted from building God's temple. You've been traumatized once, and you just can't bear the thought that it could happen again. Everything in you tells you to hunker down, to cut your losses, to settle for a little bit of happiness. So that's when you need to act counterintuitively. You need to pick up your life again and move on down the road.

You need to choose the discipline of restoration.

accept the discipline of restoration

The truth is, there are times when I'd rather do almost anything than discipline myself to do the work of recovery from a hard time in my life. But the nature of the work required for recovery can be surprising. We may not even think of these things as disciplines until we

begin to try them in the wake of a trauma. Then w
intention and effort are involved in:

- *Discipline #1: Hope.* The discipline of hope
  involves saying yes to your restoration and actually asking for what you need. It also involves
  choosing hope as an attitude when it's far removed
  from what you're actually feeling.
- *Discipline #2: Trust.* It's always a conscious choice,
  a true discipline, to remember what you know of
  God's character and to hold on to the reality that
  God sees you. During hard times, it's even more
  of a challenge, but it's the key to experiencing
  God's comfort. The Psalms often speak of God as
  a refuge, a hiding place. But you can't experience
  this great gift unless you choose to trust Him.
- *Discipline #3: Waiting and watching.* This involves
  listening in stillness, waiting on the Lord, trusting His timing, actively looking for the signs
  of His presence and His activity. (The signs are
  there, but they can be subtle and easy to miss,
  especially when we're hurting.) For me, this kind
  of watchful silence is sometimes the most strenu-
  ous discipline of all.
- *Discipline #4: Honesty and transparency.* In the
  aftermath of trauma, that could mean shouting
  at God and telling Him how you feel. It can
  mean refusing to put on a happy face or to insist

that everything is all right when it isn't. There are certainly times when you need to control your feelings for the sake of others. But your restoration absolutely depends on finding a place to confess your honest thoughts and feelings—at very least, in prayer, in a journal, or with a few friends who are close to you.

- *Discipline #5: "Controlling the wild horses."* I love the way my friend Emily Davis, who has endured more trauma than most people I know, describes this. She's referring to that tendency we all have, but trauma victims have more than most, to let our vain imaginations[13] run away with us. If we give in just a little to fear and panic and worry, those emotions can quickly take control of our lives. So while we need to be honest with our feelings, we also must stay alert to the ways our thoughts can run away with us and learn to rein in the runaway thoughts.

- *Discipline #6: Obedience instead of instinct.* Our instincts can serve us well in the early moments of trauma. A "fight or flight" response could actually save our lives in an accident. But as we move from survival toward restoration, our instincts can begin to get in the way of what God wants to do with our lives. Your instinct may be to pull away and withdraw when you need to press in to relationships ... or to hang on too tightly when you need to let people make their own mistakes. Because I am an active, "can-do" type of person, I tend to rush in instead of waiting on God's timing. But I'm learning (slowly!) that obedience has to trump instinct in this, too. We have to act on the light we're given, do what we know to do. And all this takes both courage and discipline.

- *Discipline #7: Forgiveness.* This is perhaps the most difficult of the disciplines … and the most healing. It's not something you can accomplish all at once or something you can do without God's help. But the more you move toward forgiveness, the more you free yourself to move forward in your life.

- *Discipline #8: Gratitude.* This means simply looking for signs of God's presence in our lives and resolving, by an act of will, to give thanks in all things.[14] Doing this even when it feels forced or artificial has a way of opening our eyes and shifting our perspective to see what God is doing.

- *Discipline #9: Modeling faith and integrity.* This absolutely does *not* mean faking a faith, covering up doubts, or sacrificing our integrity to our witness. But it's good to realize that the way we live our own restoration can have a powerful impact on other people's relationships with God. The more honestly and trustingly we can walk, the

more integrity we manage, the more we confess
our mistakes but accept forgiveness … the more
others will be blessed and helped.

accept the gifts that trouble can bring

I believe very strongly that some of God's greatest gifts are given in
the wake of our deepest trauma. I've experienced that in my own
life, and I've heard it from others who told me their stories.

God's gifts are always extremely personal, tailored specifically to
the needs of the recipient. They cannot be demanded or controlled.
And sometimes they are often appreciated best in retrospect.

I cannot tell you definitively how you will encounter God in
your times of sorrow. I can't promise that what you experience will
feel like a gift at the time.

But I can tell you that if you keep your eyes open and your
hands out, waiting on the Lord in trust and humility, you won't
find your hands empty.

Suzii Christian Parsons is one person who has come to appreciate the surprising gifts that come with trauma. It has been nearly
twenty years now since her young husband, Wayne, died of an
acute asthma attack. They had been married a year. He was the love
of her life—an athlete, a tennis pro. She was in graduate school,
working on her PhD. They had just begun talking of starting a
family, something Suzii had longed for all her life.

Then one day, following a tennis tournament, Wayne simply
collapsed and couldn't be revived. He was dead at age thirty.

In the years since Wayne's death, Suzii has finished her degree and become a professor. She has remarried and become the mother of two small children. But she is still acutely aware not only of the scars she carries from the trauma of bereavement but of the gifts she has received along the way. Here are just a few of the gifts she describes:

- *Gift #1: Presence.* In the midst of wrenching pain, Suzii remembers being vividly aware of the fine line between this world and the next. She remembers a powerful sense of being guided, even of being "prayed through"—praying prayers she didn't know to pray and receiving the answers in the next moment. She describes it as "just that connectedness that I don't think we're usually aware of, but when we're down in that depth we became aware of it."

- *Gift #2: Need.* When trauma brings us to our knees, when we come face-to-face with our own helplessness and our inability to make our lives work—that is often when we start to sense God working. Suzii says, "For me, when I could not control God, then I could rest in God. When you are that lost and helpless in the dark, all you can do is focus on the light."

- *Gift #3: Time.* God is gentle and kind; He lets us change a little at a time. He lets us move forward in small steps, in our own way (and asks that we grant similar grace to others who are struggling). Today, many years after the trauma of Wayne's death, Suzii describes how the acute pain of missing him has softened to a kind of wistfulness: "I find myself wishing that Wayne could know my children. They're very much Joe's children, and he's a wonderful daddy. But I do feel sad that Wayne doesn't know my kids."

- *Gift #5: Redemptive people.* Suzii recalls so many people who ministered to her in the days and weeks after Wayne's death—a great-aunt whom she barely knew, who sat by the bed when she was afraid to close her eyes; friends who knew just what to say when she called them with the news. And she realized years after her husband's death that three or four of her closest friends—those who have seen her through every step in life—had first been friends of Wayne's. She reflects, "The nature of our friendship is a gift in the wake of his death."

- *Gift #5: Being able to be a redemptive person.* During the past few years, Suzii has found herself walking more than one friend through the death of a husband. "When this first happened, I asked God, 'Are You kidding? I so don't want to be back there.' Well, God said, 'Tough.' And I have been incredibly blessed, though I've had to work at it. I've had to remember to call her every week and to check in with her, and that wasn't always easy. But then she'd write a note and say, 'I was almost gone that week, and then you called.' It's just a gift that I've been given that has nothing to do with me. I've also seen my friends discovering their own gifts and their own strength—those are just direct gifts of such horrible loss."

- *Gift #6: What comes next.* Suzii says, "I would never wish away Wayne's death because I would wish away what happened in its stead"—her work, her current husband, and her beloved children.

- *Gift #7: A less fearful perspective.* "I try to protect my kids, but I also know that even if the most horrible thing I could imagine happened—which is something happening to one of my kids—I would go on. And that there would be incredible blessings in the wake of that. Those blessings are an integral part of it, and I think that is part of the perspective I can provide for my kids, too. That all living things die, but it's not the end of the world. And blessings abound, and grace abounds."

- *Gift #8: Grace-filled surprises.* Suzii goes on: "It's not as trivial as 'Hey, don't sweat the small stuff.' Sometimes stuff is big. But it's not the end. And the lesson of it, though, is that grace is there. That in the very worst, God is always right there with wonderful gifts. And around the darkest corner, there's a marvelous surprise that you never even dreamed of."[15]

To Suzii's list of gifts that can come to us through trauma, I would add one more: the gift of disillusionment. Quite literally, trauma shatters our illusions. It reminds us that this world isn't safe, that everything we've accumulated on earth can be wiped out in a second, that life is fleeting and brief. We might already know those things—and if we read our Bible we've certainly been warned. But once we've been hit by a life-changing trauma, we absolutely *know* that these things are true. We've seen them acted out before our very eyes.

And how is that a gift?

It's a gift because it's always better to live closer to the truth, and the truth about this fallen world is part of the picture. Bad things— even very bad things—do happen, and often God doesn't intervene the way we expect. But the other half of that truth is encapsulated in Jesus' statement the night before He died: "In this world you will have trouble. But take heart! I have overcome the world."[16]

This is the fundamental truth of the God who sees us, the gift of truth we can find in the midst of our pain if we choose to look for it and open our eyes to receive it. Simply put, it's this: God sees better than we do. His vision is far broader and deeper and higher than we could ever attain, and He will do whatever is necessary to accomplish what He means to do with the world and with our lives.

The more clearly we can manage to see that—to adopt a perspective based on truth and not illusion—the more we'll be able to understand and accept God's gracious and surprising gifts.

a witness to restoration

I experienced a specific kind of grace-filled surprise during the past few years, following a time of unrelenting trauma in my life. In the process, I believe I've gotten a clearer view of the subtle and powerful ways God can handle my pain and move me toward restoration. It's one of those grace-filled surprises that opened my eyes even wider to see the God who sees me.

It had to do with my attitude toward men.

Now, if you had asked me five or six years ago if I had a problem with men, I would have told you—emphatically—no. I respected men. I liked men. Some of my best friends were men.

And yet …

I had just gone through a drawn-out, extremely painful divorce I'd never dreamed would be a reality—truly the biggest trauma in my life. I had some unresolved issues (I know now) from my family of origin. I tended to gravitate to other women who had been mistreated by men, and this probably reinforced a growing cynicism about the opposite sex. It wasn't unusual for our "venting" about our traumas to turn into less-than-honorable conversations about men. And I talked to my daughters a *lot* about being "independent." I didn't want them to be too idealistic about the security that men seem to represent to other women. I didn't want them to give their hearts too easily.

When I look back now, I realize I might have had a few *teensy* problems relating to male human beings. But this wasn't something I actively prayed about or sought intentional healing for. I really didn't understand I needed it.

But God did. And in the course of a single year, He used men to send me one healing grace after another.

The first demonstration of grace involved a man who had almost been my husband. Back in our early twenties, we were engaged to be married. But we both struggled with selfishness and immaturity, and our breakup wasn't our finest moment. Over the years, I've had many regrets about the way we ended our relationship. Mutual friends had told me that Matt[17] was happily married and that he had grown to be a fine man, but I hadn't actually heard from him since we parted ways.

Then one birthday, out of the blue, I received an ecard from Matt. I found it in my inbox—beautiful scenery, lovely music, a Scripture, and a sweet message: "I pray for the mercy and grace of God to fill your life."

I wasn't prepared for the torrent of emotion that ecard unleashed in me. I pondered its message for days, wondering how—or whether—to respond. Finally I sent him a very casual, superficial email thanking him and asking how his life was going. We corresponded a bit, very casually. Then I began to sense the Holy Spirit urging me to write a more serious email.

It took me a long time—and a fair amount of fear and trepidation—to do that. But I finally wrote and asked his forgiveness for my willfulness and immaturity, the foolish choices I had made when we were together. I told him he didn't need to respond, that I was doing this for my own healing and in obedience to the Spirit. But he did respond, and his response was full of mercy. "Tammy, I forgive you," he wrote. "And I ask you to forgive me."

That *really* opened the floodgates. I remembered more things I had done, and I wrote again, asking forgiveness for those, too. He responded with a message that is still inscribed, word for word, in my heart.

"Ask me as many times as you need," he said. "I forgive you. My heart's desire is to tell you that you're forgiven. Please keep asking it until you're certain."

I can't tell you how deeply those words touched me, what healing they unleashed in my soul. All those years, I had been dragging around such shame and failure and pain, thinking I had left them behind. I may even have blamed Matt for the burden.

What a relief to be able finally to process that early episode, to find peace and reconciliation and God's word of grace. Did I still have regrets about that failed relationship? Absolutely—probably more so now that I saw what a quality person I had left behind. But Matt's words rang in my heart with the resonance of God's grace. I really had been forgiven—by Matt, yes, but also by Someone whose heart's desire is to say, "I forgive you, and I will tell you that as many times as you need to hear it."

So that was one experience that started unraveling my complicated issues with men. The second came not long afterward with a letter from my big brother—my only brother—with whom I had not shared a true relationship in twenty years. We'd argued over a number of issues and finally reached the point where we barely spoke, other than superficial conversations at family gatherings.

Then, after nearly twenty years of strained relationship, Dean wrote me an incredibly gracious email. He asked my forgiveness for what he had said and done to hurt me. He expressed sorrow for the pain I was going through and let me know he wanted to help my family in any way he could.

That email struck me as absolutely miraculous—not just in its content, but in its timing. I have long said that timing is God's primary link to this dimension, and He was proving that in my life. Just as a primary relationship in my life was falling apart, He was restoring one I had lost twenty years earlier.

Interestingly enough, in the midst of all this, my father started reaching out to me as well, in a very intimate and personal way. Dad, now in his mideighties, is of a generation that shows love more through faithful provision than through tender words. He always expected excellence from all of us, and when I was growing up, he had sometimes seemed stern and emotionally remote.

But now, in this same year, my father began writing me beautiful handwritten letters. He expressed a new kind of tenderness, a loving acceptance that was just what I needed from my daddy. In the past few years, our relationship has grown immeasurably—a wonderful testimony that it's never too late to grow and change.

And then, thank God, came our little Cohen. When I first learned Mackenzie was pregnant, the news felt like just one more blow, more evidence of the dysfunction in our lives and my failure as a mother.

But what a blessing this little boy has been for our family! That thick, luxurious golden-brown hair. That irresistible smile. The way he softens our conflicts and keeps us focused on what's important. The way he makes us laugh.

The timing of Mackenzie's pregnancy hasn't always felt like a blessing, though God has redeemed her circumstances many times over.

And Cohen himself? Cohen has been pure blessing. Pure, unadulterated grace.

And then, in the midst of all these changes with men, these gentle shifts that were gradually moving me away from my bitter response to trauma in my life, I came to know Jerry. As I have said, it took me a little while to accept his gentle wooing. Even when I understood what a treasure he is, stepping into another marriage took a *lot* of prayer and then what felt to me like a gigantic leap of faith. Now, looking back, I can only marvel at the amazing gift of grace Jerry has been to me and my entire family—an extravagant gift from the God who sees me.

So what has been the upshot in my life from all these experiences?

I certainly felt loved by God when all this was happening. I wasn't blind to this healing of old wounds, the joy of restored relationships. But I didn't realize until I looked back that I was also losing my cynicism about men. With one redemptive encounter after another, God was gradually dissolving a clot of bitterness toward the opposite sex that I didn't even know was there.

As a result, I have a deeper sense of relating to God as my Father and Christ as my Brother. My respect for my son, Sam, as a young man has grown, and I hope I'm a better mother to him as a result. I am better able to appreciate the wonderful, God-given differences between men and women. And bit by bit, I am losing the gut-level distrust that sometimes made me prickly or overly independent.

And what a surprise all this has been! I've sent up plenty of prayers for healing in the aftermath of one of the biggest traumas of my life. But gently, quietly, in the middle of it all, the God who sees me—and sees so much more than I'll ever see—was also granting prayers I never even knew to pray.

God wins

The grace of this restoration and the wonder of God's precise timing still boggle my mind.

I hope they boggle yours too.

I hope they give you hope and courage to hold on through your trauma and its aftermath, to not despise small beginnings, to actively look for God's surprises and His timely work even—or especially— when pain touches your life.

I hope this understanding gives you a sense of the road ahead, of what you can expect as you walk the long, crooked road back from the trauma in your life.

I have no idea how it will all work out for you or those you love.

But God does. And I am absolutely certain that, through it all, He will be there for you.

He sees your heart.

He sees your need.

He is closer than your next breath.

And even while you slog through the pain of your daily life, the unseen God is working behind the scenes and in His own timing to bring about your restoration.

I was reminded of this once again when I stood in my friend Mona's bedroom, doing what I could to comfort her in her pain, feeling entirely inadequate in the face of so great a loss. Just as I was leaving, I passed her bathroom and saw it.

I had to look twice.

In large marker print on the bathroom mirror were words that Mona had written months before:

> Your children are His and not the Devil's, and you can make a case for them before the throne of God. We have the power and authority Satan does not. God provides for His children, and we are His children. For I have no greater joy than to know my children are walking in truth. God knows the end of this story, and His children win.

Standing there amid the dark, lingering fog of fear, doubt, pain, and not knowing, I saw. I saw Him. I saw His promise. I saw that He had given my friend a gift long before she knew how desperately she would need it. She still had to walk through her grief. But from the larger perspective—God's perspective—both Mona and her beloved son had won. We all win … because we are His.

Though the battle rages on and the dark fog of life circumstances threatens to engulf us, nothing escapes His watchful eye. Nothing can take us out of His hand. Our names are written on His palm. No suffering or trauma on earth can separate us from His love.

Wherever you find yourself today, my friend, whatever you carry, He sees you.

And if you are His, no matter what happens … you win.

chapter seven

see and be

Then those "sheep" are going to say, "Master,
what are you talking about?
When did we ever see you hungry and feed
you, thirsty and give you a drink?
And when did we ever see you sick or in prison and come to you?"
Then the King will say, "I'm telling the solemn truth:
Whenever you did one of these things to
someone overlooked or ignored,
that was me—you did it to me."

Matthew 25:37–40 MSG

It happened back when I was in my twenties, but I've never forgotten it. Some days the memory still haunts me.

I was working as a flight attendant, and I had a layover in Portland, Oregon. Christmas was on its way, so I decided to use my limited layover time to shop in the downtown area. I was running from store to store on a cold, drizzly afternoon, trying to put a dent in my Christmas shopping. I crossed the street toward one last department store before heading back to my hotel. And right outside that store, beside the big revolving doors, I saw a homeless man sitting quietly on a piece of cardboard.

He was dirty, disheveled, and missing both legs. And he was staring at me. He looked desperate and a little scary. He definitely made me uncomfortable.

In a hurry to finish my shopping, I entered the revolving door. But as I slowly pushed it around, I glanced in his direction, and his eyes met mine. I gave a passing half-smile, looked away quickly, and kept on pushing toward the emotional safety of the store.

I rode the big escalator up to the floor I needed and moved on to accomplish my to-do list. But as I bustled through the various departments, I felt a nudge in my spirit. I'd experienced that kind of nudge before, but this one came with words that surprised me:

This is a test. This is only a test.

What in the world? Those were the words I sometimes heard on TV prior to a civil-defense drill. But clearly they meant something else now—something involving that homeless man I had just seen outside the door. Somehow I knew that God was asking me to push past what I was comfortable with, past what I could understand, and give that homeless man money for lunch.

Oh yes, I knew those words were from the heart of God. He said, *Tell him I love him, I see him, and I care for him deeply.*

I didn't really want to do it. I must have gone up and down the elevator five times, changing my mind. But I just couldn't shake

the conviction that I needed to go out there, so I finally headed
to the door. As I pushed back through the circular glass enclosure,
the homeless man met my eyes again. It was as if he knew I would
return.

I fumbled in my purse and blurted out, "Hi, my name is Tammy,
and I just wanted to give you some money for lunch." I pulled out a
ten-dollar bill and handed it to him. "Oh, and God told me to tell
you He loves you and He sees you."

The man reached up to take the money. "I saw you go into the
store," he said. "God told me you'd be the one to help me today."
He continued to stare at me with piercing eyes and spoke with such
persistence. "But what you have to know is that this was a gift for you
from God. Because this was only a test."

My jaw dropped. "What did you just say?"

He repeated it: "This is only a test."

I can't remember if I answered him or not. I do know I turned
away quickly, my mind replaying what he had said and how he'd said
it. The whole experience seemed so strange—and it was about to get
stranger. Because as I stepped onto the busy street, only feet from
where this man huddled, I turned to look at him one more time.

And he was gone. Vanished. No trace of him.

Now I was so shaken I could hardly walk. I looked for him up
and down the street. He wasn't there. And I had only looked away
for an instant. He couldn't have walked away, and there had been no
time for someone to carry him.

I crossed the street and spotted a Salvation Army kettle ringer.
"Where did that man go?" I asked. "The one who was sitting over
there?"

The ringer shrugged. "I've been here all afternoon, and I never saw anybody over there."

So I was left wondering, just as I wonder today: Was I seeing things?

Was that man really there?

And what exactly *was* the test?

Today, looking back, I'm still not exactly sure what happened. But I do have a pretty good sense of *how* I was being tested.

It's the same test you and I face every time we encounter one of our fellow humans beings—the test of how we choose to see them and what we do in response.

Will we choose to look through God's eyes at the people we encounter daily? Will we see them—really see them? Will we enter into their reality, understand their need, and act accordingly?

It's a test of perception and response:

Will we *see* Jesus in others?

And will we *be* Jesus to them?

seeing and being

It is true that we can't really see as God sees. We don't have it in us to observe anybody from God's all-knowing eternal point of view. Our vision is always flesh dimmed and sin warped, fogged up by our very humanity.

And as for being Jesus, none of us comes close. Yes, we're made in God's image, and if we've accepted Him into our lives, He actually lives within us in the form of the Holy Spirit. But we're not

God. We're not *supposed* to be God. Managing the universe is so not our job. Redeeming the world is not our job. We're not here on earth to save people from their sins, to judge them or control them. When we try—and we do try, unfortunately—we actually fall into sin.

And yet ...

When Jesus was on earth—when His disciples could see Him with their physical eyes, hear Him with physical ears, touch His shoulder, smell His essence, taste the food and drink He handed them—He was already talking about these times when such a physical encounter would not be the way He worked in the world. And He made two things clear about the way His followers were to live in that world and relate to others.

First, when we encounter others, we are in some way encountering Him. At the very least, we are encountering someone God sees and loves the same way that He sees and loves us. We are not only invited but commanded to shift our perspective and see these other people as God sees them and respond to them as though they were Jesus Himself.

Remember the parable of the sheep and the goats, where Jesus painted a verbal picture of the final judgment? In that story, we see the glorified Jesus separating people to be rewarded or punished just as a shepherd would separate his sheep from his goats. And the favored group, the "sheep" who receive the eternal reward of a life well spent, are those who noticed the needs of others and acted to meet those needs. "Whenever you did [that] to someone overlooked or ignored," says Jesus in the story, "that was me—you did it to me."[1]

I can't think of a clearer perspective shifter when it comes to our encounters with others. We are to see Jesus in others because, in some mysterious way, He really is there.

And He's in us as well. That's the second thing Jesus taught about the way we encounter others, and it, too, is a mystery.

Jesus dwells within us and has chosen to reveal Himself through us, in our lives, in our words, and in our actions. In that sense, every time we act the way He would, we are showing people the face of the Father and standing in the place of Jesus. That's integral to our mission as Christ's followers, the one He mentioned when He prayed for His disciples the night before He died:

> I pray for them … for those you gave me,
> For they are yours by right.
> Everything mine is yours, and yours mine,
> And my life is on display in them.[2]

That's true of all of us who have said yes to Jesus. We've agreed to be His agents in the world—His hands, His feet, His voice, His heart. To *be* Him in a practical sense to the people we encounter on a daily basis.

every person you meet

Let's look a little more closely at this double mystery—that the way we see and respond to others is intimately tied up with the way we see and respond to God. When we choose to see Jesus in others and respond accordingly—treating them the way we would treat Him if He was there in the flesh—we are actively participating in the miracle of God's kingdom coming on earth.

But exactly who are we talking about when we talk about these "other people"? And what exactly are we supposed to see in them?

The Bible is actually pretty explicit about this. We're told, for one thing, that God has a special interest in the poor and the needy. He has a tender heart for orphans and widows[3] and for prisoners.[4] He cares about strangers, for those who are alone.[5] In short, all those folks that most of us tend to overlook, to write off, or to fear and shy away from. All those people that society doesn't see, God notices. He wants us to notice them too.

We're also told that we are to look on the people we meet every day as "neighbors,"[6] to be aware of their needs and even to love them as much as we love ourselves. I don't know about you, but that can be a real perspective shift.

And that's exactly where it starts—with changing the way we see. Frederick Buechner puts it so beautifully:

> When Jesus comes along saying the greatest command of all is to love God and to love our neighbor, he … is asking us to pay attention. If we are to love God, we must first stop, look, and listen for him in what is happening around us and inside us. If we are to love our neighbors, before doing anything else we must *see* our neighbors. With our imagination as well as our eyes, that is to say like artists, we must see not just their faces but the life behind and

within their faces. Here it is love that is the frame
we see them in.[7]

But it's not always that simple, is it? Some people are easy to see
and to understand, easy to love. Some people invite our compassion
and make us want to reach out. But what about these?

- that woman at work who just won't stop talking.
- the pushy phone solicitor. (Okay, you can't literally
  see her, but you definitely encounter her!)
- the guy on the corner, holding up a "will work for
  food" sign.
- the tattooed, pierced teenager hanging out at the
  coffee shop.
- the kid who beat up your kid at school.
- the ditzy teen who just cut you off in traffic because
  she was texting while driving.
- the frumpy, middle-aged woman ahead of you in
  the grocery line.
- the woman at the rest stop who you suspect is a
  prostitute.
- the young man with Down syndrome.
- the old woman with Alzheimer's.
- the guy who stole your identity.
- the IRS agent who audits you.
- the drunk driver barreling down the highway.
- the self-righteous Christian you encountered at the
  church you'll never, ever visit again.

- the out-of-control young mother you had to sit next to in the emergency room.
- the rude clerk who messed up your bill.
- the hotshot who always manages to make you look bad at work.
- your friends when they get involved in their own lives, then neglect you.
- your mother when she's being needy and demanding.
- your father when he's being stubborn and dictatorial.
- your husband when he's acting clueless.
- your wife when she just won't let it drop.
- your children when they push every button you have.

Every encounter with another human being brings a test. And with some of them, the test is really a challenge. Will we choose to see this person as God does? As our neighbor? As someone to love?

Can we really get it through our heads that God sees every person we encounter exactly the way He sees us?

Each one was created in the image of God and bears a divine spark within him or her.

Each one is a sinner—just like you and me.

Each one has been sinned against—just as you and I have—and bears the scars of that sin. Each one suffers and struggles in ways we probably don't know.

And every single person you and I meet is someone Jesus died for. Someone God loves passionately. Someone He wants to provide with a future and a hope.[8]

Get your mind around that. Can you look that way at every single person you meet?

Probably not. I know I fail at it all the time.

I have absolutely no difficulty seeing my husband or my kids or my grandkids or my brother and sisters that way. (Well, most of the time.) But seeing people as God does becomes an uneasy choice when it comes to the people who make me uncomfortable. People who push my buttons. People who are tiresome and boring. People I don't approve of. People who intimidate or hurt me. People I fear. People I just can't stand.

I'm sure that's true for you, too. So how do we learn to see *those* people as God sees them?

First, I'm convinced we won't be able to manage it until we understand how God sees us. We can't love others unless we know what it is to be loved. And we're going to have a hard time seeing others unless we take to heart that our heavenly Father takes notice of us and cares for us.

Second, I'm convinced we need to depend on the Holy Spirit within us to show us what we can't easily see on our own. Our human empathy and understanding can only go so far. We need Christ within us to be able to see with God's eyes.

And we won't get it perfectly, of course—not here on earth. Just as we can see God only through a fog, we'll always struggle to see other people clearly as well.

But every time we manage it, each time we shift our perspective to view another person the way God sees him or her, a little miracle happens. Maybe even a big one.

Jesus at Walmart

To get just a little sense of how that might work, I want to share a piece my daughter Mackenzie wrote in her blog:

> I met Jesus today. More than once.
>
> I had an hour or so to kill, so I decided to pick up items for school at my local Walmart.
>
> The place was insanely busy. As I walked toward the doors, I passed about twelve Walmart employees sitting on the ground in a circle. They looked tired, sad, a little dirty. Thinking about their faces, I almost collided with a runny-nosed little boy. I said excuse me. His mom yelled at him to stay closer to her.
>
> *Lord, I just wanted to get some office supplies.*
>
> Every checkout counter seemed to have a long line trailing from it. I eyed them impatiently and hoped that by the time I wanted to leave there would be an open lane.
>
> In the office-supply area, trying to decide between a yellow folder and a blue one, I felt a stare. An elderly woman in front of the tape display was looking at me through oversized glasses.
>
> *I agree, lady. What the heck am I doing at* this *Walmart?*
>
> She was overweight and smelled like a nursing home. An oxygen tank hung over one

shoulder. I tried to keep from staring back as I studied the folders. She turned and started down the aisle. I noticed that she was alone. No one held her hand or helped carry her oxygen. She walked with a limp.

What if this was your grandma, Mackenzie?

Ah yes … and then You speak, Lord.

"Um, is there anything I can help you with?"

She stared at me again and had to think about her words. "I can't reach the masking tape," she mumbled and then half smiled at me with no teeth. "I was going to find a clerk.…"

"I'll be happy to grab that for you." I handed her the masking tape and gave her a big smile. She told me her husband had just passed away and she needed to pack up many of his belongings. She began to limp away again. I told her to have a blessed day. She turned back and shook my hand.

Okay, Lord. I'm listening.

I gathered all my items and headed to check out. There was only one station without a huge line. I hurried to stand behind a mother with two kids.

No wedding ring. Stripper boots. Skinny as a rail. She looked so lost and so broken. Her small children were in one cart. Another cart was piled with groceries.

I stood behind them quietly as the clerk scanned item after item. The mom kept dropping coupons, money, keys. I believe I bent over three times to help her pick up something. She was frazzled, out of it, and kept eyeing the world around her as if she knew she was being judged.

The total came to almost a hundred dollars. She counted out a huge stack of ones and fives and found she was three dollars short. She rolled her eyes and told the clerk to put back the milk.

"Hey, no worries," I said. "I'll spot you."

She eyed me suspiciously. "If you knew what it's like to be a single mom, you'd understand that I don't need your charity. I just left the rest of my money at home."

I was shocked and hurt. But I proceeded to tell her I did understand. "I've been a single mom too. And I just want to pay for the milk—for your kids. That's it."

She hesitated, then finally nodded.

I handed a five to the cashier, whose face had turned bright red. The mom nodded again as he handed her the receipt.

"God sees you," I told her. Then she was gone. Just like that.

I paid for my items and left the store that was full of snot-nosed kids, neglected elderly people, poor families, single mothers, frazzled hearts.

I prayed for the people I had encountered that
day—that they'd see Jesus in what happened.
Not religion. Not church. Not pity or charity.

But Jesus.

Just as I saw Jesus in them.[9]

That's exactly the kind of miracle I'm talking about: the miracle that happens when we make the choice to see Jesus and to be Jesus. The ordinary becomes extraordinary. Everyday human interactions become sacraments. And those words we're always praying—"Thy kingdom come, Thy will be done on earth as it is in heaven"—become a reality right in the midst of our ordinary lives.

why doesn't it happen?

Which leaves us to wonder: Why doesn't this perspective shift happen more often? Why don't we try harder to see others as God sees them or to be Jesus to them?

One reason is busyness. We are so very busy. We're too busy to stop, to notice, too busy with the ongoing needs and demands of our lives to see as God sees or embody Jesus in the world.

Another big reason is fear. We fear we'll look foolish. In certain circumstances (and certain parts of town), we may fear physical harm. More often, though, we fear that our lives will be disrupted. We fear we'll be asked to do more than we can do. We fear that we'll have to change (we probably will) or that we'll be rejected or judged.

We fear we won't do or say the perfect thing, and so we become paralyzed.

Another common reason, I'm afraid, is simple selfishness. We like our lives the way they are. We're preoccupied with taking care of what we have or getting more. We're focused on our own needs and problems and reluctant to care for anybody else's.

And our compulsion to be in control, which underlies so many other sins, is also a factor here. I mentioned earlier that I love to give God a good idea. And I've noticed that when that happens—when I fall into thinking I'm the one in charge—very little loving actually gets done. Instead of stepping into people's lives in Jesus' behalf, I tend to step back and order people around, to criticize and find fault, to proclaim what needs to be done without actually doing it.

And all too often, we fail to see because … we just don't see. Like the people Jesus healed in New Testament times, we're blind and deaf and mute and crippled—spiritually if not physically. We need our eyes opened, our ears unstopped. We need to let ourselves be touched, to breathe in the reality of others' presence and need.

Most of all, I believe we need to have our hearts softened—in the biblical sense.

In the Bible, God is always urging His people not to harden their hearts.[10] And I don't think He's merely saying, "Don't be hardhearted or cruel." He's talking about our willingness to pay attention to what He is doing in our world and to participate in it.

Jesus made this clear in Mark 8, when the disciples complained about not having any bread. He had just fed five thousand people in front of their very eyes, and they were worried about not having any lunch! So Jesus said, "Why are you talking about having no bread? Do you still not see or understand? Are your hearts hardened? Do you have eyes but fail to see, and ears but fail to hear? And don't you remember?"[11]

"Don't you get it?" He was saying. "Don't you see what I'm doing here? You need to pay attention because I want you to be part of this."

That's exactly what He asks of us today—what He wants to help us do.

"Today, if you hear his voice," another Scripture urges (it could just as well be "today, when He shows you a neighbor's need") —"do not harden your hearts."[12]

Instead, open your eyes. Obey the nudge as best you can. (What to do is clearer than you'd like to admit.) Choose to act on behalf of the God who sees you, who sees and loves all His children and wants us to love and care for one another.

See ... and be.

how not to be Jesus

When we encounter another person, we always have a choice about how to respond to him or her. And sadly, not all our typical responses are the kind that reveal Jesus to the world.

For instance, it's so easy to look away instead of really looking at the people around us. We focus our attention on ourselves—what we need to do, how busy we are, how little money we have, how difficult our lives are at the moment, what important issues need our attention. I've done this way too many times, and I'm sure you have too. It's basically the same response as the lawyer and the Pharisee who hurried by the wounded man in Jesus' story of the Good Samaritan.[13]

Even more commonly, I find, we can respond to those we encounter with judgment and criticism—by keeping our eyes on the other person's sins and shortcomings. We choose to give our opinions rather than acknowledging our common humanity. And even if we would never do this out loud, we may do it mentally—assuming we know what made them what they are or what they should be doing or what's going on with them.

It's so easy to fall into doing this on a little or a large level—to categorize people on the basis on what they're wearing, what they look like, how they act, what we believe they may be thinking or doing. Because our vision is limited, it's all too easy to jump to conclusions. And when we do that, we forget to see and be. We need the reminder of a quote that I've seen so often on the Internet, attributed to a number of people: "Be kinder than necessary, for everyone you meet is fighting some kind of battle."

Another possible way to respond to other people, especially people in need, is to patronize them—to help them without truly seeing them. It's absolutely possible to give to others or serve them without actually loving them. It's possible to interact without engaging—without actually entering other people's reality or paying attention to what they actually need. When we do that, we miss the opportunity to really see other people and to show them Jesus' heart.

A very common substitute for truly seeing someone is to try to change the other person, to basically offer our help and attention in exchange for the other person's response. This is another way of making it all about us—our opinions, our requirements. We attempt to assert control by laying down ground rules. We'll give money … *if* it's used for food and not alcohol. We'll invite someone over … *if* that person invites us back. We'll help others … *if* those others are properly grateful. This, too, misses the point of seeing Jesus in others and being Jesus to them.

Now, this last issue can be a little tricky because in some cases we do help another person by holding him or her accountable for change. But in my opinion, this is only appropriate if we've earned the right to do that by becoming fully engaged in the other person's life, and only if we do it with the other person's permission.

It's just so easy to miss out on the chance to see Jesus and be Jesus to the people we encounter. But we don't have to miss out. We always have another option. The option to open ourselves to the Holy Spirit's nudge and obey the commands of Scripture. The option to open our eyes and our hearts and hands. To see Jesus in others. To be Jesus to them.

the choice to bless

How does that translate into daily reality—into our everyday experience of encountering other people at home and at work and at church and, yes, at Walmart? I'd like to suggest a few possibilities.

A good first step, of course, is to say a prayer and ask for guidance. Actually, prayer is a good step at every point along the way. It's not a bad idea to pray silently, *Lord, You have brought this person to my attention. What are You trying to show me? What do You want me to do now?*

The answer may be just a small gesture. That's so important to keep in mind because it frees us from all our fear of being overwhelmed and overextended. Remember, we're called to play a part in what God is doing at any given moment. It's God's job to redeem the world. Our job is to represent Him in the world and do His work with His guidance and power. As Joni Eareckson Tada so eloquently puts it:

> The Christian faith is meant to be lived moment by moment. It isn't some broad, general outline—it's a long walk with a real Person. Details count: passing thoughts, small sacrifices, a few encouraging words, little acts of kindness.[14]

So your first call when you encounter another person may be simply to acknowledge him or her. This can be as simple as eye contact and a nod or a smile or another brief, friendly gesture. In some circumstances, the touch of a hand can make all the difference. In other cases, a gesture such as my ten dollars to the homeless man might be appropriate. What matters is the small choice of turning your eyes toward another person instead of away—of connecting rather than disconnecting.

I learned recently that the Zulu equivalent of "hello" is *sawubona*. But that doesn't just mean "hello." It literally means "I see you." And the proper response, *ngikhona*, means "I am here." And behind those greetings, apparently, is the sense that if we're not seen, we don't even exist.[15]

I believe we can learn a lot from that little language lesson. Simply greeting someone—really seeing that person and conveying that you see him or her with a simple gesture—can make such a difference. Just a warm hello or a nod and a smile—an acknowledgment of our shared humanity—can convey the same powerful message of "You exist. You matter ... because I see you."

That simple act of connection can be amazingly powerful if it's given as a gift without judgment. Denver Moore, a former homeless man turned insightful author, comments on both the power of a simple act, which he calls a "blessing," and the potential to sully the blessing with judgment:

> The thing about it is, though, gifts is free. When you give a person a gift, you is also givin' that person the freedom to do whatever they want with it. When you give a homeless man a dollar, you ain't sayin', "Here. Go buy yourself a chicken." If you really wanted him to have some food, you'd take him in the McDonald's and buy him a Big Mac and a apple pie.
>
> No, when you give a homeless man a dollar, what you really sayin' is, "I see you. You ain't invisible. You is a person." I tells folks to look at what's written on all that money they be givin' away: it says "In God We Trust." You just be the blessin'. Let God worry about the rest.[16]

In some cases, a greeting may stretch into a brief encounter, a small conversation. And this, too, can be both surprisingly simple and amazingly powerful. When there's something to be said that brings life and hope and healing and faith and trust and encouragement—especially "God sees you!"—we need to be very intentional about actually speaking it.

Along with the words, of course, may come an opportunity to help—just as Mackenzie helped the elderly woman in Walmart. I'm not talking here about a big investment of time. I'm talking about taking a minute to respond to an immediate need—to bless another by opening a door or picking up a dropped item. Just a little act of blessing that says, "I see you. I noticed you. You exist, and that makes a difference to me."

the choice to share

There will be times, of course, when the appropriate response to really seeing another person will call for a little more than a greeting or a simple conversation. In some cases, for instance, it will be appropriate to give something of material value—to share our personal wealth with another. The book of 1 John states this specifically: "If anyone has material possessions and sees his brother in need but has no pity on him, how can the love of God be in him? Dear children, let us not love with words or tongue but with actions and in truth."[17]

And yes, I'm talking about money here. I don't think it's a coincidence that Jesus taught more about finances than on any other single subject. God brought up the subject about 2,350 times in His Word.[18] Apparently, He's more concerned about how we manage our material blessings than He is about how piously we pray or how much faith we can muster up—even more than how we behave sexually.

Why? I think it's partly because how we handle our money and possessions reveals our perspective on life and reflects the way we see things. In fact, Jesus specifically related vision to money in His Sermon on the Mount:

> Your eye is a lamp for your body. A pure eye lets sunshine into your soul. But an evil eye shuts out the light and plunges you into darkness. If the light you think you have is really darkness, how deep that darkness will be! No one can serve two masters. For you will hate one and love the other, or be devoted to one and despise the other. You cannot serve both God and money.[19]

Did you ever notice that those famous verses about money come immediately after those verses about vision? The juxtaposition of those verses was a little confusing to me until I read that "pure eye" and "evil eye" are Hebrew idioms meaning "generous" and "selfish." I like the way Rachel Olsen explains it:

> A pure eye is an eye that sees the needs of others and is willing to meet them. Likewise … an evil eye is an eye that ignores the needs of others in favor of taking, having, and holding for oneself. It's the green-eyed greedy gut who runs around eating the world up.…
>
> If we're not compelled to live generously, it's because we've got an "eye problem," a vision

problem. We've lost sight of who God is and what He does. We've forgotten the mercy of His salvation, the grace of His presence, not to mention the blessing of His divine savings plan. If we aren't interested in depositing treasure in heaven, we've lost sight of the fact that this world—and all its treats and treasure—is temporary....

Oh, that Jesus ... would help us unfurl our fists, and begin living open-handed—trusting God to provide both for and through us.[20]

I've been both humbled and instructed by the example of my husband, Jerry, in this regard. Both in times of plenty and in harder times, I've seen him notice needs—a kid trying to make it through school, a family with medical bills—and open up his hand in response, sharing generously. And the good that he does with the money he gives springs not only from the financial resources but also from the fact that he has noticed the need.

Seeing and giving must go hand in hand, or giving becomes nothing more than a financial transaction. And I would add that it's a good idea to actually ask what is needed instead of assuming we know. Elizabeth Buchanan makes this point graphically when she describes the huge pile of junk on the outskirts of the Romanian orphanage where she volunteered:

Broken refrigerators and cars and old televisions and God knows what else are all up there. Why? Easy. *Someone donated them.*

When a donation truck rolls up to the orphanage, it's full of things that the organization needs—furniture, blankets, etcetera. It's also equally full of other junk that the donor just needed to get rid of and write off on their tax returns. The orphanage can't turn away the junk without turning away the whole truck and they can't afford to turn down *anything*. So, they pick out what they can use and send the rest up the hill. The summer I was there they were trying to sell some of the stuff for scrap, but I'd bet anything that most of it is still up there on that hill. Rusting.[21]

Giving materially is important—vitally important. It is the means by which we feed the hungry and clothe the naked. It can connect hearts and give a powerful message of "God sees you, and so do I." Seeing and being involves giving generously, openheartedly, out of our abundance and even in our need. (Jesus made that clear when He saw the widow giving her mite in the temple.[22])

But when we can give, if we want to be Jesus to others, we first need to pay attention. We need to see before we can be.

the choice of hospitality

Your encounter may take you beyond simply donating goods, of course. You may be called to offer hospitality to someone you meet. And I don't just mean inviting that person over for coffee or a dinner party—although that might be a possibility. I mean actually welcoming people into your life and even into your home.

Does that idea make you a little nervous? That's true for many participants in my hospitality workshops. They long to be welcoming, but they find the idea intimidating—usually because they have the wrong idea about what hospitality means.

Hospitality isn't the same as "entertaining"—not at all. It's not doing something unusual for "company," but creating an everyday lifestyle that provides welcome to family, friends, strangers … and yourself. It's using all the resources God has provided—your physical space, your possessions, your time and energy and talents, your unique family background and personality, even your failures and mistakes—to extend comfort and care to other people. It's using your unique gifts to make them feel safe and comfortable and wanted—to give them a positive message about their value.

Quite literally, hospitality is choosing to love people with your whole life.

Stop for just a minute and consider just how powerful that idea really is. Loving people with your life. Serving them in a way that is uniquely yours. Offering your very self as a refuge to those who feel alien and alone (and doesn't everybody feel that way sometimes?).

This kind of hospitality is not just for those with gorgeous homes, professional cooking skills, support staff on call, or special spiritual gifts. It's the way God specifically commands us all to live. That's right: From the first books of the Bible to the last, we are repeatedly commanded to "practice hospitality"[23] in our homes, our churches, and our lives—to welcome strangers and welcome one another as well. Hospitality is for every follower of Christ.

And no, it's not always easy. The practical skills of hospitality are learned by doing—quite literally "practicing" hospitality. They take a certain amount of time and effort, although not nearly as much as some people think. But I guarantee that every effort you make at opening your heart and your home to others will pay a dividend of joy.

Can you tell that hospitality is a personal issue with me? It's something I care about deeply, because I've seen the difference it can make in people's lives. Good things—even miraculous things—seem to happen when we invite people into our lives and homes, and especially when we eat together. We learn so much about serving others and caring for them on an intimate, personal level.

Remember when some of the disciples encountered Jesus on the road to Emmaus after His resurrection? They didn't even recognize Him until they invited Him for dinner. Only when they broke bread together did they see who He was.[24]

And that, in my mind, is the true gift of hospitality. When we open our lives and our homes to others, when we invite people to break bread with us in the spirit of the living God, everybody gets a little glimpse of the way things were meant to be. Around the table, serving one another, is a perfect opportunity to meet the Lord Jesus—both to see Him and to be Him.

the choice to help

There may be times when you feel the nudge to do more than just greet or bless the people you meet or to welcome them occasionally into your homes. You may be called to move into another person's life and commit yourself to him or her at least for a season, to help that person on an ongoing basis and develop a real relationship. This is a big step and needs to be bathed in prayer, but it can be a transformative experience.

One of the best-known examples of this kind of relationship is that of Ron Hall, a Texas art dealer, and Denver Moore, the former homeless man I quoted earlier. If you haven't read their book, *Same Kind of Different as Me,*[25] I wholeheartedly recommend it. It's the story of how Ron's wife, Deborah, brought these two *very* different men together while Denver was still living on the streets and how she nurtured a relationship that is still changing lives. Deborah has since passed away, but Ron and Denver still live together, travel together, speak and write together—mostly on the subject of how we can see Jesus in one another and be Jesus to those we see.

A friend of mine developed a similar relationship with a woman she met at church, someone who was struggling with multiple physical, emotional, and crushing financial challenges. My friend drives the woman to doctor appointments and to the grocery store, helps her financially, and just tries to look out for her. She tells me she's had similar commitments in the past, but I had to smile when she told me, "God gives me people to help, but He knows what I can manage, so He only gives me one at a time."

Another dear friend, Lynn Brown, and her husband, Steve, have honed this "one at a time" philosophy into a fine art, a ministry of mentoring young women who are in need of a little extra help getting launched. Lynn and Steve nearly always have someone living in their spare bedroom. Steve uses his gifts as a financial planner to help "their girls" learn to budget and manage their lives; Lynn mostly listens and mothers them and "just loves on 'em." (Did I mention that Lynn is *very* Southern?)

In my own experience, these kinds of helping relationships have tended to follow the season of my life. Before my children were born, my first husband and I invited another family to move in with us—in a tiny apartment—while they struggled to get back on their feet financially. Later, when my kids were small, I "adopted" one of their friends whose mother was struggling and had little time for her only child. I took that girl to church with us, invited her for meals and overnights, and did my best to include her in our lives. We lost touch with that little girl when her mother moved. But we've recently reconnected via Facebook, and I'm thrilled to say she's grown up to be a lovely young woman. She's told me that my decision to invest in her life at a vulnerable time showed her a lot about what life could be.

I can't tell you when or if you might be called to be Jesus to someone in this special way. I can tell you that if you say yes, you'll probably be deeply challenged and deeply blessed. You'll learn a lot about yourself, about relationships, and about obedience.

start simply, but simply start

Are you feeling a little overwhelmed by now? I know I've had times when I've felt helpless in the face of all the need I see around me, paralyzed by the sheer size of the challenge. There are so many people who are hungry and thirsty and sick and in prison, so many who feel unnoticed and unwelcome and alone. And I'm just one person. There's a limit to how much I can see and be!

But God knows that. He knows each of us better than we know ourselves—our gifts, our limitations, and our specific role in bringing about His kingdom. God doesn't want us to be all things to all people, in other words. He wants us to pay attention to the person He's placed in front of us. He wants us to connect instead of disconnect, to love instead of looking away.

And He never expects us to do it alone. Not only do we have Christ in us, but each of us is also part of His body on earth, His church. When we function as we're meant to, we serve together, support one another, reach out together. That's what we're there for—to help one another see Jesus and to combine our gifts to collectively be Jesus to the world. (We also have the privilege of seeing Jesus in one another and serving our fellow members of the body.)

We are never called to do everything for everybody all the time. In fact, much of the time, we'll be called to be lovingly obedient in small but still challenging ways. To help the elderly woman in Walmart. To speak a kind word to the person next to us in line. To take a break from our shopping to buy lunch for a homeless man. To respond in love to the needs that God puts before us.

You don't have to do it all. You don't have to take care of everybody all the time. You can do what I tell the women in my hospitality workshops: *Start simply, but simply start.*

Don't worry about all that needs to be done, in other words. Just concentrate on obeying the nudge of the moment, meeting the need that's right before you. Don't try to do everything. But do something. And trust your heavenly Father to show you the next thing you need to do.

It all becomes easier if you remember who you are—and who God is. You can't save the world. You can't even save one other human. All you can do is extend love to those you see. The rest is up to God. That means you don't have to worry about how people respond to your acts of love. You don't have to worry about how they see you. All you need to worry about is pleasing the God who sees you and loves you and wants you to love His other children.

what God likes to see

I have four children. All but one of them are out of the nest now, and my baby, Mikia, is just about to fly. But at one time in my life I was a caretaker of four little ones under six. At another point I had four teenagers in the house at once. So I know a little about how brothers and sisters get along.

I've seen squabbles and knock-down-drag-out battles. I've heard a lot of verbal sniping. There have been times when one kid wasn't speaking to another or when another kid was holed up in his or her room. We've had jealousy and judgment, cut-downs and criticism. And as a mother, I always hated to see that kind of thing. It hurt when my children didn't treat one another right.

But oh, how wonderful it was in our house when everyone got along! I've always loved to see my kids work and play together, helping one another, supporting one another, and enjoying one another.

As they have grown and matured, it's been a joy to watch them become friends and not just siblings.

I love nothing better these days than to just sit in a room with all my kids—when I can get them together in one place—and watch them talk and joke. And to know that, if any of them runs into trouble, they'll have one another's backs.

Don't you imagine that God feels that way too?

Don't you think He loves it when the children He made, the children He sees and loves, manage to see and love one another, too?

I believe that. I believe it's a great joy to Him when we make the effort to see one another, to bless one another, to share with one another and welcome one another into our lives and offer help to one another.

Because God the Father, the God who sees us all, just loves it when His children play well together.

chapter eight

living in the light

I have come into the world as a light,
so that no one who believes in me should stay in darkness.

John 12:46

I'll call her Rebecca.[1]

She's a young woman who recently contacted me because she was struggling with a big secret in her marriage—something she didn't feel she could share with anyone she knew. She had read my book *Confessions of a Good Christian Girl* and thought I would understand and could help her. I agreed, because I know that lonely, isolated feeling of being trapped in the darkness of a reality you don't dare to reveal.

What was Rebecca's secret? The truth emerged gradually, over the course of several sessions.

At first, she told me that her husband, an associate pastor in their church, had been looking at Internet porn "the last few weeks." She had found out by accident and didn't know what to do. Should she confront him? Talk to someone in the church? Just pray and wait to see what would happen?

Then, after we'd talked a while, she revealed a little more. It had actually been more than weeks. She had known and agonized about her husband's porn addiction for months, even years. He had promised to stop and had even succeeded for a while. But he always gave in again. Rebecca kept stumbling over one little time bomb or another—the evidence that her husband was deeply involved in Web porn.

Eventually, Rebecca confessed to me, she had fallen into the habit of *looking* for evidence. She'd learned to track her husband's computer usage. He'd used various tools to hide his surfing. She'd learned to circumvent those methods. The whole issue had become a kind of cat-and-mouse game between them, a source of constant pain to both.

And then the latest bomb went off. Rebecca discovered that her husband wasn't just viewing online porn. He was also connecting with other women online through email, instant messaging, and escort sites. That's when she came to me. She was pretty sure that he hadn't actually met anyone yet, but she was afraid he would eventually do that.

She was afraid, period. The web of secrets in her home was rapidly shutting off the light in her life. And she had no idea what to do with any of it. She didn't trust her husband to change. She didn't dare tell anyone at church and risk her husband's job. And she didn't want to leave her husband. She loved him. But she felt like she was gradually collapsing under the weight of their secrets.

back to hide-and-seek

Rebecca is not the only person trying to steer her way through a minefield of secrets. Most of us have realities that we hesitate to bring to church with us or share with casual friends. Many of us, in fact, live with secrets we hardly dare whisper even to ourselves. We may have spent our whole lives tiptoeing around whispered mysteries, untold tales, urgent cautions, and complicated rules about who can be trusted with our secrets and who can't. Our secrets are what keep us playing hide-and-seek with God and with others.

If we want to keep our eyes on God, to enjoy a real and healthy relationship with the One whose very nature is light, we're going to have to do something about our secrets.

That doesn't mean we'll necessarily tell all our secrets to everyone. But it does mean we need a major perspective shift on what we're hiding, why we're hiding it, and what all that hiding is doing to our lives and our relationship with God—who sees it all in the first place.

We explored some of this in chapter 1. But now I'd like to bring this book full circle by looking more deeply into ways that our secrets keep us in the dark ... and the choices that can help us step out of hiding into the presence of the God whose very nature is light and truth.

how we hide

The hows and whys of our hiding are as many and varied as our individual circumstances and personalities.

We hide our secrets through denial—burying them so deep we aren't even consciously aware of them. We do it by avoidance, setting issues aside and refusing to deal with them, "at least for now." Sometimes we surround our secrets with a wall of silence, refusing to talk about them, or we use our authority to forbid others from revealing them. We may protect our secrets by compartmentalizing—placing various aspects of our life (family, work, sex) in separate mental boxes and convincing ourselves that one has nothing to do with the other. We may rewrite history, rearranging the facts and retelling the new story often enough to obscure the truth. We may even resort to outright lies and force others to lie as well ... all to protect the secrets no one else can know.[2]

Some secrets are big and explosive. ("Don't tell anyone what Grandfather did to you!") Others are relatively minor. ("Don't tell the boss I'm taking off early today.") Groups of people may keep secrets from one another, creating a complex web of alliances. But certain groups may also band together to keep secrets from the outside world.

We typically hide events, attitudes, and feelings that might reveal our weaknesses or cause someone—especially us—discomfort or embarrassment. We also hide realities that might trigger rejection or condemnation, loss of social status or financial standing. The particulars may change according to the era, our particular corner of society, or even our gender. (I've been told that men are more apt to hide feelings or financial problems, while women are more likely to hide opinions that could cause conflict.) In general, we conceal problems that make us feel vulnerable. But as we've seen, we also sometimes hide what we're doing so we can keep on doing it.

why hide?

We keep secrets out of *fear,* because we anticipate being hurt or having someone we love hurt. We dread embarrassment, rejection, being judged by others, or simply not being loved. We fear having our vulnerabilities exploited, having information used against us, and losing protection and provision. When I counsel a person struggling with secrets, I always ask her, "What are you afraid of losing?"

Guilt is a close companion of fear. We hide because we know we've done something wrong and we fear judgment or punishment. In some cases, we hide from our feelings of guilt because we just can't face what we've done.

Shame underlies many of the secrets we keep. We have a sense that we are not okay, that we are unworthy or that something is deeply wrong with us. So we keep our sins, weaknesses, and dysfunctions a secret because we can't bear to have others know what we are really like.

And *pride* is right on the heels of shame as a motivation. Pride in this sense means being too attached to our image or reputation and unable to face our failures and weaknesses. Rather than expose our problems and live with the reality of who we really are, we choose to hide behind a facade.

Not all secrets involve negative motives, of course. We may also keep secrets out of *love, loyalty,* and *responsibility.* Parents appropriately try to shield children from realities they are too young to understand—parental quarrels, financial fears, sexual issues. Children may similarly try to protect parents from their problems and their pain. A married person may keep a secret to avoid worrying or upsetting a spouse, and a good friend may guard a confidence instead of spreading it through the gossip network.

But even the secrets we keep with the best of intentions can bring us trouble if we're also trying to use them to *control* what happens in our lives. I'm convinced that this impulse to be in control underlies most of our hiding. It mixes with all our other motives.

We hide because we're afraid or ashamed, but also because we want to control what others do or think. We keep secrets out of pride, but we're also trying to control what people think of us. We suppress information to protect the ones we love but also to control our own discomfort. We may also enjoy the sense of power our secrets give us—knowing something someone else doesn't, exploiting others' weaknesses against them, getting away with something. Or we may keep secrets to avoid being controlled by others.

In other words, we hide because we want to do things *our* way.

Sometimes, of course, we hold on to secrets because we've been taught that's just the way life works. This often happens in cases where secrets have been kept for generations. Children are tutored in a culture of silence—don't tell anyone, keep this in the family, don't let anyone know. We've been raised to believe our lives will fall apart if our secrets are told or discovered.

When this happens, the secrets themselves take control.

Unfortunately, they can get us into big trouble.

the problem with secrets

I'm not prepared to insist that all secrets are harmful. Some are trivial, harmless, or merely personal—like a secret ingredient in a family recipe. Some secrets can actually bond people together (as a surprise anniversary party might do) or help define us as a group (like an inside joke or a saying that just a few people understand).

Some secrets do their job of protecting the innocent or preserving jobs, reputations, or even lives. Some are eventually rendered relatively harmless by time and cultural change. (The horrifying secret of your great-grandmother's generation, the one that would have ostracized the family from the community, may now seem relatively innocuous.) Some secrets, such as a painful confession kept confidential by the one who hears it, can actually make more room for God's grace to work.

So what's the big problem with secrets?

In the first place, *they don't always remain secrets*, and their revelation can be traumatic. The longer the secret is kept, the bigger it is, and the more public the exposé, the more pain is likely to accompany its exposure. You've seen it on TV—that deer-in-the-headlights look of a politician's spouse or preacher's wife whose mate's infidelity, criminality, or worse has been revealed in public. Those who aren't in on these secrets inevitably feel betrayed when the truth is finally told, even if the secrets were intended to protect them.

Even when they stay under wraps, *our secrets can wear us out.* Keeping the truth under wraps is like trying to hold a big beach ball under water. It eats up an enormous amount of energy that could be used for other purposes and leaves us tired and tense.

Secrets also tend to keep us stuck in our negative patterns—and the longer we hide, the deeper the ruts become. As long as we stay in hiding, our fear and shame and guilt can't be addressed … or relieved. Our pride and rebellion remain intact, and hiding becomes a holding pattern. Secrets rob people of information they may need to break old patterns. They hold us back from confronting problems. They keep those who are trying to change from obtaining needed accountability.

And by their very nature, *secrets tend to grow*. Secrets often spawn lies, and one lie leads to another. Omitting the facts in one area necessitates making up facts somewhere else. Secrets thus tend to make it difficult for us to have open relationships with people or God.

Can *secrets make us crazy?* It feels that way sometimes, especially if we're the ones on the outside of a secret. Untold secrets warp our sense of reality and undermine our faith in our own good sense, especially if there's a disconnect between the nonverbal signals we pick up and what we're told is true. People whose spouses have had an affair sometimes describe this kind of conflict between what they intuit and what they're told, what they suspect and what they want to believe. Children in a troubled family may set aside their natural sense of curiosity, because there are always things they must not ask about or acknowledge. They may even develop learning disabilities that clear up when the secret is finally revealed.[3]

Not surprisingly, secrets *can wreak havoc on relationships*. Some people in a group may connect too tightly around a secret (therapists call this "enmeshment"); some grow disengaged. Some become insiders, some outsiders. Trust and communication suffer as people hide information from one another, tiptoe around what cannot be discussed, or whisper secrets that cannot be told. Relationships thrive on a healthy give-and-take between personalities, and secrets tend to block that flow. When we're hiding something, it's difficult or impossible to make a close connection with God or other people.

The resulting isolation makes us lonely. It also makes us a bigger target for the Enemy—because *our secrets tend to separate us from God*. Two major themes of Scripture are that God is a God of truth and that He desires an intimate relationship with us. But secrets by their very nature compromise truth and make relationship difficult. It's just hard to draw close to God when we're trying to hide from something. And this, of course, is where sin comes in—because separation from God is the very definition of sin.

I'm not claiming that *every* little secret is a sin, but in my experience, sin and secrets almost always walk closely together. Sometimes the realities we're hiding are inherently sinful. Sometimes our motives are sinful—our pride, our need to control our lives. Sometimes it's just the act of hiding—which in itself is a power play, a way of doing things our own way without turning to God.

It's been that way from the very beginning.

walking in the light

Remember Adam and Eve hiding from God in the bushes? Deep in the forest's shady darkness, the first man and woman found a place to make themselves small. And there they huddled together, devastated by their newfound fear and shame, waiting for the inevitable, trying to convince themselves it might not come.

Maybe they could hide there long enough and God would forget about them.

Maybe He had other things to do.

Maybe He couldn't even see them.

Yeah, right.

I think that's where the bickering began—the angry whispers as they crouched there in the darkness.

"How could you be so stupid—listening to a *snake?*"

"Well, he made sense. You would've done the same thing. And you didn't exactly hesitate when I shared the fruit with you."

"Don't try to put this off on me. You're the one who made the decision."

"Well, you could have stopped me."

"Why, you manipulative, controlling—"

"Shh. He'll hear you."

And so it continued—at least as I imagine it—until Adam and Eve heard a voice calling them out of their dark hiding places. The voice of the God who saw them.

The piece of fruit Adam and Eve devoured in the garden didn't just precipitate the first sin in history. It also launched the first secret. All the elements were there—the fear, the shame, the relational discord, the power plays. The rebelliousness and the squabbling. The desperate need for a hiding place.

One way or another, people have been hiding—and sinning—ever since.

But notice what happened next. I think it's important.

God went looking for Adam and Eve in the cool of the day, out in the fresh air and the soft breeze and the beautiful, golden evening light. He called out to the man and the woman: "Adam ... Eve ... where are you?"[4]

And at that point Adam actually did something right. When God called, Adam answered. He admitted what they had done. He confessed. The man and woman emerged from their hiding places, stepping out of the darkness and into the light, revealing themselves to the God who saw them.

And that, I believe, made a huge difference.

Yes, Adam and Eve's disobedience had serious consequences. The consequences were built into the very act of sin itself. Once the man and woman chose to disobey, they chose the inevitable direction their lives—and ours—would take.

But have you ever wondered what would have happened if the first man and woman hadn't made that other choice—to come clean with God? What if they hadn't answered when He called them into the light? What if they had stayed huddled in their dark hiding place?

Their punishment, I'm sure, would have been the same. But I wonder if their connection with God would have been different.

Obviously God knew what had happened—and what had to happen next. He has always been the God "from whom no secrets are hid."[5] And obviously, He was angry at what His man and woman had done. But He still loved them, still wanted to be in relationship with them. And because Adam and Eve were willing to come out of hiding and 'fess up, God would make things better for them.

He made them skins for covering and protection. He gave them necessary information on what to expect in coming days. Yes, He put them out of the garden, but He never abandoned them. We see this at the very beginning of the next chapter of Genesis, when Eve gives birth to Cain and says, "With the help of the Lord, I have brought forth a man."[6]

The moment Adam and Eve emerged from hiding, in fact, I believe God started making plans for how He would redeem the spectacular mess they had made of His spectacular creation. And I can't help but think that Adam and Eve's confession had something to do with how it all happened.

Once they made the choice to step out into the light, God had room for His redemptive work. And I believe that remains true today when it comes to our secrets.

choosing to come clean

Confession instead of hiding, truth instead of secrets—the choice can make such a difference in our lives. As I see it, that's the way things work in this fallen world.

When we keep things hidden, they almost never improve.

When we bring them out in the light, God has something to work with.

The problem is, that's counterintuitive for most of us. We're so used to operating out of fear and shame and pride, so accustomed to trying to control our lives, that our instinct is just like Adam and Eve's. We want to cover up, to keep our secrets. We want to jump into the bushes and hide and, maybe, drag others in there with us.

I know that impulse because I've done my share of hiding.

For much of my life, I thought of myself as a pretty open person. I'm naturally outgoing and friendly. My family raised me to value truth and integrity. Sure, I had my issues, but I was basically honest—or so I thought.

Then life happened to me. Sin happened to me. And one day I realized that my "open and honest" life was stuffed with secrets— secrets I couldn't stand for people to know.

I was a good Christian woman, after all. I *liked* having people think of me that way. I hated to admit that anything negative was going on behind the scenes. So I swept my issues under the rug. I denied my problems, sometimes even to myself. I insisted on pretending I was the kind of person I wanted to be, even when the signs were clear that I was nothing of the sort.

It took me a long time—and a lot of pain—to reach the point where I wasn't willing to hide anymore.[7] But I finally relaxed my hold on my "upstanding" image and started to listen to God—to actually listen for His word in the midst of all my secrets and my dysfunction.

And God's word for me, as it was for Adam and Eve, was, "Where are you?"

God's word was, "I'm out here in the sunshine. Why don't you come out from your hiding places and walk with Me?"

I heard His voice through those amazing words from 1 John:

> God is light; in him there is no darkness at all. If we claim to have fellowship with him yet walk in the darkness, we lie and do not live by the truth. But if we walk in the light, as he is in the light, we have fellowship with one another, and the blood of Jesus, his Son, purifies us from all sin. If we claim to be without sin, we deceive ourselves and the truth is

not in us. If we confess our sins, he is faithful and
just and will forgive us our sins and purify us from
all unrighteousness.[8]

I've read that particular passage of Scripture over and over during
the past few years, and I really believe it's a key to our hide-and-seek
dilemma of longing yet fearing to be seen. And I don't think it's just
a matter of confessing sin, though that's a big part of it. I think it's
about a whole different approach to what happens in our lives. Once
again, it's about choosing to "live by the truth." It offers the key to
freedom from the secrets that keep us trapped.

Simply put, the thing to do when we've been hiding in the dark
is make the choice to step into the light. To move away from our
secrets, to push the branches aside and purposely reveal ourselves
instead of hiding our faces. We face up to our secretive, controlling, self-protective, deceitful ways and the way our secrets warp
and damage our lives. We admit that those secret, controlling, self-
protective ways are hurting us and others, isolating us, trapping us
with fear and shame. We actually name the problem to ourselves
and to God and to at least one other person, someone safe and
carefully chosen, who can be trusted to keep a confidence and not
respond with judgment. We agree to what God already sees and
then give Him room to work.

That's where the confession comes in. We lower our guard, venture into the sunshine, and take a step toward living by the truth.

Once we make that commitment, once we dare expose our
secrets to the light, things start to open up. God states specifically
that if we dare come out of hiding, He'll take care of the rest. He is

faithful. He is just. He takes care of our sins, forgives us freely, cleans us up, and sets us free. Isaiah 43:25 assures us He does this "for [his] own sake." He does it because of who He is and because He wants to have a relationship with us—what an amazing thought!

There's no need to keep lying to cover up other lies, no more worrying that our secrets will blow up in our faces. Our painful memories get a chance to heal. We can finally draw closer to God and to other people without our secrets getting in the way. We're poised to move toward a more whole and integrated existence. And we're freed to share with others what it means to live boldly and freely in the light of God's grace.

As we choose to unveil ourselves, we actually unveil the God who sees us as well.

the trouble with confession

Does that all sound too simple?

It *is* simple. But you probably already know it's far from easy, especially when other people are involved in our secrets. It's hard to come clean with God about our personal sins and secrets. And what about secrets we share with our spouses, our siblings, our children, our close friends?

How do you confess sins that involve other people, anyway? How do you reveal what someone else wants to keep hidden or won't even acknowledge? How can you open up secrets when you're not even sure what the truth is? Do you tell the whole truth as you see it and risk destroying the people you love?

To get more specific, do you tell your spouse you've had an affair?

Do you turn your best friend in to the authorities for drug use?

Do you confront your elderly parents about your dysfunctional childhood?

Do you tell your son that his father isn't really his father?

Do you go on national TV with any of this or blog it for the world to see?

Well, the answer to that last question is fairly obvious—though not to everyone, judging by what I see on TV and the Internet! If hiding almost always involves sin, our efforts at telling the truth can be sinful too.

Even so, I believe God calls us to a far more rigorous honesty and openness than most of us are comfortable with. After all, He is the way, the *truth,* and the life. He desires *truth* in our "inner parts." He sees what we keep secret and "brings hidden things to light." And He calls us into the light as well … because, as we've seen, "in him is no darkness at all."[9]

The Bible is clear that God wants us to come out of hiding and trust Him with our hearts, our reputations, the well-being of those we love. He wants to forgive us so we can have full fellowship with Him. And He wants us to live just as openly with others so that we all can heal, enjoy intimate relationships, and live with freedom and confidence instead of fear and shame.

But here's the twist that's easy to miss: Although God calls us all to live openly in His light, He calls us *one at a time.*

That means I'm not called to confess my husband's sins … or my children's, my friends', or even my deceased great-grandmother's. I'm not called to expose their secrets, force their decisions, or make their choices for them, even if I believe the choices I want them to make would improve their lives.

Living in the light, in other words, doesn't mean I'm honor-bound to tell everything I know to everyone I meet. It doesn't mean I can't guard my privacy or that I have a right to violate someone else's. In fact, if I find myself with a strong urge to set people straight, tell my side of things, or "make sure the truth comes out," that's a pretty good sign I'm hiding from my own issues and *not* living in the light of God's truth.

Living in the light doesn't even mean I won't have any more secrets—at least not from other people. The Bible tells us clearly that there is "a time to be silent and a time to speak,"[10] and the Old Testament is full of stories about heroes who hid, acted in secret, or even lied outright. Jesus often went places in secret and for a long time cautioned His disciples not to tell people who He was. He also very famously instructed His followers to do their giving and praying and fasting in secret to avoid the temptations of pride. After Jesus' resurrection, the early church often found it necessary to hide from authorities and meet in secret ... even while they went about the task of spreading the gospel.[11]

To me, all this confirms that there are times when it's better to keep our mouths shut and our secrets unrevealed. How can we tell when this is the case? The following questions have helped me decide in times of doubt—though I've learned that it's possible to twist or rationalize any one of them. That's why it's important to rely on the Holy Spirit for day-to-day (sometimes moment-to-moment) guidance.

- *What is prudent?* It really isn't safe or wise to share certain realities in certain arenas—or to certain people.
- *What is the right time to reveal secrets?* Sometimes patience is a wiser strategy.
- *What might the consequences be?* Have I counted the cost of revealing a secret?
- *Whom should I tell?* Who can be trusted? Who needs to be protected?
- *Whose secret is it?* Each person is responsible for his or her own heart and relationship to God.
- *What are my motives?* Is there a hint of vengeance, bitterness, or glee in my truth telling? Do I hope to get an edge in some dispute?
- *What is God saying to me?* Prayerful listening always helps.
- *Most of all … what would love do?* Because isn't love God's ultimate criteria?

a policy for living in the light

I'm still struggling with what all this means in relation to my own secrets. As events continue to unfold in my life, I still find myself torn by how much is appropriate to share and how much I should to keep to myself. I know my personal light is limited, my capacity for denial and self-deception is high, my urge to control others and protect myself is strong, my trust in God prone to waver.

I'm still tempted sometimes to run and hide from God and from others. I'm still tempted to reveal what makes me and my family look good—or at least interesting—and to downplay what puts us in a bad light. And then, when I do come out of hiding and reveal myself, I'm often tempted to drag everyone else into the spotlight with me. I sometimes feel a strong need to point out the sins of those who have hurt me, to justify myself at their expense, to confess things that aren't really mine to confess.

At the same time, I have made a commitment, a kind of personal policy, to openness and transparency—or what twelve-step groups call "rigorous honesty"— rather than secrecy and hiding. To the best of my ability, I choose to live the kind of life that David P. Gushee described when he wrote: "Truth is not simply something that is believed or even spoken. Rooted in faith in the trustworthy triune God, truth is a way of being, a path that is followed, and a place that one inhabits."[12]

In other words, I've chosen a policy of living in the light for me and for my family. And I feel called to be as honest and transparent in my ministry as possible, consciously unveiling myself to reveal God's work in my life. I believe it's that policy that brings people like Rebecca to me, that encourages others to come out of hiding as well.

I'm finding, however, that the particulars of my policy will vary. How much I reveal varies. Whom I reveal it to—and when—varies a lot. This is the place I'm trying to inhabit for now:

In my relationship with God, I am trying to commit to absolute honesty. I stop hiding from Him (knowing He sees me anyway), and

I give Him conscious permission to shine His light into the corners of my being, to show me what I'm concealing. I come to Him in confession and ask His forgiveness for the ugly and painful things He brings to light. In so doing I recognize that there will be an ongoing process of revelation—partly because I keep on sinning, partly because He is gentle and patient and reveals my hidden realities as I am ready to handle them.

In my relationship with myself, I'm trying to come to terms with my capacity for self-deception and tainted motives and my difficulties in seeing the big picture. I'm trying to trust God enough to be humble and teachable, to back off from defensiveness, to welcome the downfall of my denial. I may not always be compelled to tell everything I know, but I am committed to telling myself the fullest truth possible.

In my family relationships and my very close friendships, I'm trying my best to relate with honesty and openness, "speaking the truth in love,"[13] keeping in mind my responsibilities and my limitations, trusting God to make up the difference. And I'm trying to establish an atmosphere of openness with those I care about, admitting my faults and mistakes, encouraging honesty in others, showing to them the accountability and grace that I receive from God.

In my public relationships, I commit to as much transparency as I can possibly manage. But I am also committed to respecting the privacy and choices of those I love. So I'm trying to learn to confess honestly, but confess only what is mine to confess or what I have permission to share. I'm working to lay down my compulsion to defend myself and make myself look good—allowing God to be the keeper of my reputation instead.

For me, this means I combine my rigorous commitment to honesty with a rigorous—and for me, rather novel—commitment to keeping my mouth shut when appropriate. It means I try to refrain from offering my opinion and judgment of what others should do—unless they ask, or unless they're my children or someone whose growth I'm responsible for. (As my children pass into adulthood, I refrain even more from telling them what to do—or at least that's the idea.) When possible, I also try to refrain from justifying myself and telling my side of a story when I'm misjudged, especially if giving my side would result in telling someone else's secrets.

I don't have any of this down perfectly. I'm still prone to get into a conversation and blurt out something that's just not my business. (To avoid this, whenever possible I try to decide *ahead of time* what I'm going to tell about a situation.) I'm still susceptible to coloring a story in a way that makes me and my family look good and others look less than stellar. I'm still guilty of telling secrets that are not really mine—sometimes as a way of covering up my own sin. ("Brutal honesty" about some secrets can be quite an effective cover for the other secrets we *really* don't want anyone to know.) I'm still known to "protect" those I love with half-truths or silence when I'm really only protecting myself. And I'm still tempted from time to time to set the record straight on misleading gossip about me that I happen to learn about.

But here's something interesting I'm learning as I endeavor to keep my commitment to light-filled living.

First, I'm learning that it brings me closer to my family, my friends, my church family, and God. There really is less fear, less shame, more freedom. When I've been honest about myself, I find myself trusting others' love for me. I don't have to live in fear that something I've kept hidden will be found out and others will reject me because of this knowledge.

At the same time, I find that living in the light gives me a healthy independence. I'm not as clingy, not as needy, not as driven by my fear and shame and pride and control issues. I'm no longer trapped and constrained by the need to cover up my failures and challenges. And because I trust the God who sees me, I can loosen my grip on what I want people to know and leave myself, my loved ones, and my reputation to His dependable care.

Best of all, I find that my choice to live transparently encourages others, including other members of my family, to be transparent with me. They can see me as I am—a vulnerable human being who is struggling as they are, not a lofty or idealized image of myself—and they can relate. When I show them love or talk about grace and hope, they're more inclined to listen or even confess their own painful secrets, as Rebecca confessed hers to me. What a privilege to have the light of Christ shining *through* me!

I find that living in the light is an ongoing—and challenging—adventure. There's always that temptation to step back into the shadows and let fear or pride have the last word. Thank God for His mercy and grace as I learn what it means to leave the bushes behind and step out into the golden light of God's presence.

I want that for you, too. So I'm inviting you to join the adventure.

Let God shine His light not only on your hidden sins and secrets, but on your essential loveliness—your *loved-ness*.

Let Him shine a light on others you meet so you may see them the way He does.

Let Him shine a light on your circumstances, so you can see them with a broader view and a truer perspective.

Let Him shine a light on the goodness of His creation and the power of His redemption, so you can accept these great gifts with joy and gratitude.

Let Him shine the light of His eternal light so you can see … the God who sees you.

the Father's love letter

How do we know what God sees in us? He's told us so, over and over, in His Word. I love this beautiful collection of Scripture paraphrases, collected in the form of a love letter, that sum up God's heart toward each of us:[1]

My Child ...

> *You may not know Me, but I know everything about you* (Ps. 139:1).
> *I know when you sit down and when you rise up* (Ps. 139:2). *I am familiar with all your ways* (Ps. 139:3). *Even the very hairs on your head are numbered* (Matt. 10:29–31). *For you were made in My image* (Gen. 1:27). *In Me you live and move and have your being* (Acts 17:28), *for you are My offspring* (Acts 17:28). *I knew you even before you were conceived* (Jer. 1:4–5). *I chose you when I planned creation* (Eph. 1:11–12). *You were not a mistake, for all your days are written in My book* (Ps. 139:15–16). *I determined the exact time of your birth and where you would live* (Acts 17:26). *You are fearfully and wonderfully made* (Ps. 139:14). *I knit you*

together in your mother's womb (Ps. 139:13) and brought you forth on the day you were born (Ps. 71:6).

I have been misrepresented by those who don't know me (John 8:41–44). I am not distant and angry, but am the complete expression of love (1 John 4:16). And it is My desire to lavish My love on you (1 John 3:1), simply because you are My child and I am your Father (1 John 3:1). I offer you more than your earthly father ever could (Matt. 7:11), for I am the perfect Father (Matt. 5:48). Every good gift that you receive comes from My hand (James 1:17), for I am your provider and I meet all your needs (Matt. 6:31–33). My plan for your future has always been filled with hope (Jer. 29:11) because I love you with an everlasting love (Jer. 31:3). My thoughts toward you are countless as the sand on the seashore (Ps. 139:17–18), and I rejoice over you with singing (Zeph. 3:17). I will never stop doing good to you (Jer. 32:40), for you are my treasured possession (Ex. 19:5).

I desire to establish you with all My heart and all My soul (Jer. 32:41), and I want to show you great and marvelous things (Jer. 33:3). If you seek Me with all your heart, you will find Me (Deut. 4:29). Delight in Me and I will give you the desires of your heart (Ps. 37:4), for it is I who gave you those desires (Phil. 2:13). I am able to do more for you than you could possibly imagine (Eph. 3:20), for I am your greatest encourager (2 Thess. 2:16–17).

I am also the Father who comforts you in all your troubles (2 Cor. 1:3–4). When you are brokenhearted, I am close to you (Ps. 34:18). As a shepherd carries a lamb, I have carried you close to My heart (Isa. 40:11). One day I will wipe away every tear from your eyes (Rev. 21:3–4), and I'll take away all the pain you have suffered on this earth (Rev. 21:3–4).

I am your Father, and I love you even as I love My Son, Jesus (John 17:23), *for in Jesus, My love for you is revealed* (John 17:26). *He is the exact representation of My being* (Heb. 1:3). *He came to demonstrate that I am for you, not against you* (Rom. 8:31), *and to tell you that I am not counting your sins* (2 Cor. 5:18–19). *Jesus died so that you and I could be reconciled* (2 Cor. 5:18–19). *His death was the ultimate expression of My love for you* (1 John 4:10).

I gave up everything I loved that I might gain your love (Rom. 8:31–32). *If you receive the gift of My Son, Jesus, you receive Me* (1 John 2:23). *And nothing will ever separate you from My love again* (Rom. 8:38–39). *Come home and I'll throw the biggest party heaven has ever seen* (Luke 15:7).

I have always been Father, and will always be Father (Eph. 3:14–15). *My question is … Will you be My child?* (John 1:12–13).

I am waiting for you (Luke 15:11–32).

Love, your Dad,
Almighty God

The Father's Love Letter, used by permission, Father Heart Communications. Copyright © 1999–2010 www.FathersLoveLetter.com.

an ongoing conversation

questions for thought and sharing

chapter one: please see me!

1. Read Hagar's story in Genesis 16 and 21. Does anything surprise you about the story? Explain.
2. Describe a time or times in your life when you felt forgotten, ignored, rejected, or simply invisible. Do you ever feel that way now?
3. Describe a time or times when for some reason you became aware that someone else felt unseen. What did you do?
4. Is the idea of "God sees me" always comforting or reassuring to you? Why or why not?

5. Describe a time or times when you knew—really knew—that God saw you.

6. What are some of the ways you tend to hide from yourself and others?

7. What would it take for you to say, "I have seen the God who sees me"? What would it take to share this message with someone else?

chapter two: the God who sees

1. Can you think of a little gift or "godwink" you've experienced in the past few months that reminded you that God does see you? What happened? What are some ways you could be more aware of God's presence?

2. Many of the "names" used for God in the Old and New Testament—such as El Roi—were really titles or descriptions of one aspect of God's character. (For more information, check out the websites listed in the notes section.) What additional names would you give to God, based on your personal experience of Him?

3. Describe a time in your life when you just couldn't understand what God was doing or why. Do you feel like you understand better now, or is it still a mystery? Do you think being able to understand better would bring you closer to God?

4. The Bible says that Jesus was tempted "in every way." What do you think this means? Do you find it encouraging? Disturbing? Both? Do you think Jesus was *really* tempted to sin? Explain.

5.   Describe a time when you saw God's work only in retrospect.

6.   Referring to this chapter and your own experience, write out a word portrait of God similar to the one in 1 Corinthians 13. Who is God to you? How do you feel about knowing that this God sees you?

chapter three: what God sees in you

1.   List the nine things this chapter points out that God sees in you. (Hint: look at the subheads.) Can you think of some more? Which of these means the most to you?

2.   List five things you like about yourself and five things you don't like. What is the one characteristic you'd most like to have recognized or appreciated? Is there a part of you that you wish God *couldn't* see?

3.   Name a time when you believe you disappointed God or missed His calling—either accidentally or on purpose. Why do you believe that?

4.   What are some mistaken ideas you have had in the past about the way God sees you? What changed your mind or your view?

5.   Try my experiment for a day. Use a marker to write the name of someone you love on the palm of your hand. What is your takeaway from this experiment?

6.   Can you think of a time when you believe God put you in a certain place at a certain time for a reason?

chapter four: choosing a miracle

1. This chapter states, "Sometimes the greatest miracle is just a perspective change" and goes on to say that, in a sense, you can "choose a miracle." How do these ideas resonate with you? How do they compare or contrast with your sense of what a miracle can be?

2. What would you say is the most important epiphany of your life? Can you think of a time when you longed for an epiphany and it didn't happen?

3. Have you ever experienced the miracle of a perspective change? To what extent was this perspective shift a gift from God? In what ways was your intentional choice involved?

4. What are some areas in your life where you tend to be blind and in need of healing? (This could be something that you've become aware of or that someone has told you about.)

5. What are some basic beliefs you use to filter your experiences and help you see? Do you think the idea of "believing is seeing" could be dangerous or misused?

6. Where in your life do you tend to go to encounter God? Can you name a time when you were surprised by encountering God in an unexpected way?

7. In what ways could a shifted perspective on God change your prayer life? The way you do your job? Your family relationships and your friendships?

chapter five: blind time

1. Describe a time in your life when, no matter how hard you tried, you couldn't "see" God. What helped you through that time? Do you think you learned anything? If so, what did you learn?

2. "I believe one of most important reasons God hides Himself from us is that He wants us to seek Him." What are some of the ways that you seek Him (or want to seek Him) in your own life? How can you know that you have "found" God?

3. How do you respond to the idea of "do what you know to do"— that is, follow God without special instructions? Why do you think so many people have trouble heeding that simple advice?

4. If I were to ask you, "What is the next thing you believe God wants you to do?" what would your answer be?

5. Can you think of a time when your "vision" was blocked because you failed to obey God? What happened?

6. Tell a story of a time when you couldn't see what God was doing, but later you could see how He was working things out for you.

chapter six: when bad things happen

1. What discussions have you heard about the "problem of evil"? What answers have been most helpful to you? What questions in this regard still haunt you?

2. What has been the most traumatic experience of your life? What experience do you fear most?

3. Visualize Jesus standing right next to you during a past time of deep pain or trauma. What feelings does this exercise bring up in you? Comfort? Resentment? Explain.

4. Why do you think some people feel closer to God in times of trial and some people feel more distant? What makes the difference?

5. Which of the "disciplines of restoration" listed in this chapter do you find most challenging? Which ones are easiest?

6. God told the prophet to ask Zerubbabel, "Who despises the day of small things?" What are some ways this could play out in stressful times? What "small things" are you most likely to despise?

7. Looking back on your life, can you think of any times when the unseen God was healing or restoring you without your even knowing it? What happened?

chapter seven: see and be

1. What kinds of people do you have the most difficulty seeing Jesus in? What kinds of people push your buttons?

2. Why do you think judgment and criticism are such natural responses to encountering other people?

3. What can you do when you really are too busy to stop and engage with another person? Do you think we should always have to stop and engage with people while we're working to get things done?

4. Which of the four possible responses mentioned in this chapter—blessing, sharing, hospitality, and helping—sounds

the most attractive to you? Which sounds like the biggest challenge? What do you think that reveals about you?

5. What are some practical strategies to help you "see and be" without getting burned out or overwhelmed?

chapter eight: living in the light

1. Read the book of 1 John in a translation you don't usually read (see www.biblegateway.com for a variety of translations). What do these four short chapters suggest to you about living in the light of the God who sees us?

2. What are some of the secrets you've held on to in the past and feared would be revealed? Were they revealed eventually? How did that happen? What was the result?

3. How do you think secrets and lies are connected? How do secrets become lies?

4. What, in your opinion, is the difference between guilt and shame? Do they have the same or a different remedy?

5. List some specific examples, from your own life or the lives of others, of how an urge to control can cause us to hide from the light. Do you believe attempts to control are always sinful? What makes them harmful?

6. This chapter discusses seven reasons that secrets can be problematic. What are those reasons? Can you think of any others?

7. What specific choices does this chapter say you can make to help you step into the light?

8. Have you faced any dilemmas in your life regarding what to share and what not to share? What were some of the issues? (Share these only if you're comfortable doing so!)

9. If you were to write out your own "policy" for dealing with secrets, what would it be?

10. Have you ever faced a situation where lies and hurtful words were being spoken about you? How did you respond, and what was the result? How do we let go and continue to walk in the light when something like this happens?

notes

chapter one: please see me!

1. I've kept the Mother Teresa attribution for this quote because I believe it beautifully represents her ministry. However, the official website for the Mother Teresa of Calcutta Center classifies it as "a significantly paraphrased version or personal interpretation of a statement Mother Teresa made; they are not her authentic words." See www.motherteresa.org/08_info/Quotesf.html#2.

2. Genesis 16:12.

3. Genesis 16:8.

4. Genesis 16:11.

5. Genesis 16:13.

6. Angela Thomas, *My Single Mom Life: Stories and Practical Lessons for Your Journey* (Nashville: Thomas Nelson, 2007).

chapter two: the God who sees

1. For a helpful description of God's many biblical names, see www.hebrew4christians .com/Names_of_G-d/El/el.html or www.preceptaustin.org/god%27s_name_-_a_

strong_tower.htm. Or see Exodus 20:5; Psalm 23; 95:1–3; 144:1; Isaiah 9:6; 54:1; 61:10; Matthew 23:37; John 1:1; 8:12.

2. 1 John 1:5.

3. Exodus 13:21.

4. Psalm 119:105.

5. Isaiah 9:2.

6. John 8:12.

7. Matthew 5:14.

8. John 1:18 MSG.

9. Matthew 6:18.

10. Colossians 1:15; Hebrews 11:27.

11. 2 Corinthians 4:18.

12. Isaiah 55:8–9. See also 1 Samuel 16:7.

13. Isaiah 45:15.

14. 1 Corinthians 13:12.

15. Psalm 33:13–15.

16. Matthew 10:29–31.

17. Specific wording here is from "The Holy Eucharist, Rite One," *The Book of Common Prayer* (New York: Church Hymnal Corp.), 323.

18. 1 John 4:7–8, 12, 16, 19.

19. David J. Abbott, "The Facts of Love," God Loves U, www.godlovesu.com/facts_of_love.htm.

20. 2 Peter 3:9.

21. Joel 2:13.

22. Matthew 11:29.

23. Psalm 103:12.

24. John 4:24.

25. Psalm 25:10.

26. Psalm 103:14 NKJV and MSG.

27. Dennis Ngien, "The God Who Suffers," *Christianity Today,* February 3, 1997, www.ctlibrary.com/ct/1997/february3/7t2038.html.

28. Hebrews 4:15.

29. Isaiah 53:3–5, 9.

30. Isaiah 43:1–4 MSG.

31. Squire Rushnell, *When God Winks: How God Speaks Directly to You through the Power of Coincidence* (Nashville: Thomas Nelson, 2006).

32. Matthew 25:40.

33. Colossians 1:15.

34. John 14:9, author's paraphrase.

chapter three: what God sees in you

1. Amy Tan, *The Joy Luck Club*, directed by Wayne Wang (1993; Burbank, CA: Buena Vista Home Entertainment, 2002).

2. See, for example, Psalm 8:4, Luke 1:48.

3. Mary DeMuth, "He Pulled the Covers over His Son," MaryDeMuth.com, December 21, 2010, www.marydemuth.com/2010/12/he-pulled-the-covers-over-his-son.

4. Matthew 10:30.

5. Isaiah 49:15–16.

6. Psalms 149:4.

7. Matthew 7:11; Luke 11:13.

8. 1 Samuel 16:7 NASB.

9. See for example Luke 14:1–14 (healing on the Sabbath); Luke 10:25–37 (Good Samaritan); Mark 10:2–12 (divorce); John 8:2–11 (woman caught in adultery).

10. Mark 10:17–22.

11. John 4:29.

12. John 4:1–42.

13. Matthew 26:31–35.

14. "Brennan Manning Live at Woodcrest," from Woodcrest Church, Columbia, MO, posted by "toddster5," May 30, 2007, www.youtube.com/watch?v=pQi_IDV2bgM.

15. John 8:11 NKJV.

16. Matthew 14:22–33.

17. John Eldredge, *Waking the Dead* (Nashville, TN: Thomas Nelson, 2003), 33–34

18. Isaiah 46:10.

19. Jeremiah 29:11 NLT (1996).

20. 1 Corinthians 2:9 MSG.

21. Psalm 37:4.

22. Luke 15:11–32.

23. Luke 15:1–7.

24. Romans 8:14–16.

chapter four: choosing a miracle

1. Deuteronomy 29:4 NKJV.

2. See Matthew 17:1–13; Mark 9:2–13; Luke 9:27–36.

3. Acts 9:1–22.

4. Matthew 13:13–16 MSG.

5. Isaiah 55:6.

6. Don Osgood, *Listening for God's Silent Language: Hearing God Speak in the Unexpected Places of Life* (Minneapolis: Bethany House, 1995), 9.

7. For just a few examples, see Matthew 6:25–34, 10:26–31; Mark 5:36; Luke 12:32; John 14:27; Luke 12:35 (especially in *The Message*).

8. Matthew 26:41.

9. See Matthew 25:1–13.

10. Kimberlee Conway Ireton, *The Circle of Seasons: Meeting God in the Church Year* (Downers Grove, IL: InterVarsity, 2008), 118–119.

11. Matthew 5:8.

12. Luke 11:34 KJV.

13. Luke 10:41–42.

14. Psalm 46:10.

15. Isaiah 30:15.

16. James 4:8.

17. 1 Thessalonians 5:18.

18. Ann Voskamp, *One Thousand Gifts: A Dare to Live Fully Right Where You Are* (Grand Rapids: Zondervan, 2010), 35.

19. The "bread, not stones" reference is from Jesus' Sermon on the Mount, found in Matthew 7:9–11.

20. The phrase about the universe unfolding as it should is from Max Ehrmann's famous prose poem "Desiderata," written in 1927 and attributed to various other authors for many years. See Max Ehrmann, *The Desiderata of Happiness: A Collection of Philosophical Poems* (New York: Crown, 1995), 10.

chapter five: blind time

1. Leonard Sweet, *Nudge: Awakening Each Other to the God Who's Already There* (Colorado Springs: David C Cook, 2010), 75.

2. Hebrews 11:6.

3. 1 Corinthians 13:12.

4. Hebrews 11:39–40 MSG.

5. Deuteronomy 4:29.

6. 1 Chronicles 28:9.

7. Psalm 105:4.

8. Proverbs 8:17. See also Isaiah 55:6.

9. Jeremiah 29:13.

10. Matthew 7:7.

11. Acts 17:27.

12. John Piper, "What Does It Mean to Seek the Lord? Meditation on Psalm 105:4," Desiring God: God-Centered Resources from the Ministry of John Piper, August 19, 2009, www.desiringgod.org/resource-library/taste-see-articles/what-does-it-mean-to-seek-the-lord.

13. Psalm 27:13.

14. Mark 12:30.

15. Mark 12:31.

16. 1 John 1:9.

17. Matthew 6:12–14.

18. Matthew 25:31–46.

19. John 13:34–35; Hebrews 10:24–25.

20. Proverbs 3:5.

21. Oswald Chambers, "Whereby Shall I Know?" *My Utmost for His Highest,* October 10, www.oswaldchambers.co.uk/Readings.php?day=10&month=10.

22. Chambers, "Whereby Shall I Know?" *My Utmost for His Highest.*

23. Exodus 33:20.

24. Exodus 33:18.

25. Philip Yancey, *Reaching for the Invisible God: What Can We Expect to Find?* (Grand Rapids: Zondervan, 2000), 75.

26. Matthew 18:20.

27. Robert A. Arbogast, "Invisible God," Olentangy Christian Reformed Church, Columbus, OH, October 24, 2010, www.ohiocrc.org/sermons/InvisibleGod.pdf. Used by permission.

28. NKJV.

29. John 14:16–18 MSG.

30. John 20:26–29.

31. I'm indebted to my friend Anne Buchanan for this insight, which she tells me has been especially helpful in her life.

chapter six: when bad things happen

1. It's not really my purpose here to explore the issue of why God allows evil and suffering. If you want to explore it, here are a few good resources: (1) C. S. Lewis, *The Problem of Pain* and *Mere Christianity,* available in several editions, including

a combined anthology called *The Complete C. S. Lewis Signature Classics* (New York: HarperOne, 2002); (2) Martyn Lloyd-Jones, *Why Does God Allow Suffering?* (Wheaton, IL: Crossway, 1994); (3) Philip Yancey, *Where Is God When It Hurts?* (Grand Rapids: Zondervan, 1990); (4) Joni Eareckson Tada and Steve Estes, *When God Weeps: Why Our Sufferings Matter to the Almighty* (Grand Rapids: Zondervan, 1997).

2. This is a true story, but some details have been changed to protect privacy.

3. See Ezra 3–6; Haggai 1; Zechariah 4; Zechariah 8.

4. Zechariah 8:4–5, 12. See also Zechariah 4:7, 9; Zechariah 4:5.

5. Hampton Keathley IV, "Zechariah," April 2008, www.bible.org/page.php?page_id=978.

6. Zechariah 4:6.

7. Haggai 2:3–5.

8. Zechariah 4:10.

9. Zechariah 8:13.

10. If you're struggling in this area, I'd like to suggest a book recommended by my brother-in-law, Daniel Beyers, who is a licensed professional counselor dealing with issues of trauma: R. Dandridge Collins, *Trauma Zone* (Chicago: Moody Publishers, 2007). I would also personally recommend a powerful book that helped me immensely in a very hard time: Gerald Sittser, *A Grace Disguised: How the Soul Grows through Loss* (Grand Rapids: Zondervan, 2004). One book is practical and informational. The other is deeply felt, very personal, and profoundly insightful. Both can help.

11. Liza Kendall Christian, personal interview with the author. Used with permission.

12. William Ritter, *Take the Dimness of My Soul Away: Healing After a Loved One's Suicide* (Harrisburg, PA: Morehouse, 2004), 62.

13. Romans 1:21–22 KJV.

14. 1 Thessalonians 5:18.

15. Suzii Parsons, personal communication with the author. Used with permission.

16. John 16:33.

17. I have changed his name and some details to protect his privacy.

chapter seven: see and be

1. Matthew 25:40 MSG.

2. John 17:9–11 MSG.

3. For just a few scriptural examples of God's care for widows and orphans, see Exodus 22:22; James 1:27; Psalm 10:14.

4. Examples include Psalm 68:6; 146:7; Isaiah 61:1; Luke 4:16–20; Matthew 25:36.

5. Examples include Job 31:32; Matthew 25:35; Hebrews 13:2.

6. Luke 10:25–37.

7. Frederick Buechner, *Beyond Words: Daily Readings in the ABC's of Faith* (New York: HarperCollins, 2004), 27.

8. Jeremiah 29:11.

9. Mackenzie Maltby Tamayo, "8th Street Walmart," A Rainbow in Your Sky, April 24, 2010, http://mackenzietamayo.blogspot.com/2010_04_18_archive.html. Adapted and used with permission.

10. For example, Psalm 95:8; Proverbs 28:14.

11. Mark 8:17–18.

12. Hebrews 3:7–8.

13. Luke 10:25–37.

14. Joni Eareckson Tada, *Glorious Intruder* (Colorado Springs: Multnomah, 1989), 217.

15. Brian Watts, "Sawubona—What Can We Learn?" quoted in Ron Irvine, "Honoring the Soul," Living with Open Hands, December 7, 2008, http://livingwithopenhands.wordpress.com/2008/12/07/honoring-the-soul/.

16. Ron Hall and Denver Moore, *What Difference Do It Make?* (Nashville: Thomas Nelson, 2009), 70.

17. 1 John 3:17–18.

18. "Money and Possession Scriptures," Crown Financial Ministries, 2005, http://denverchurchofchrist.org/crown-financial-documents/108-2350-scriptures-on-money-and-possessions/download.html.

19. Matthew 6:22–24 NLT (1996).

20. Rachel Olsen, *It's No Secret: Revealing Divine Truths Every Woman Should Know* (Colorado Springs: David C Cook, 2010), 102, 104.

21. Elizabeth Buchanan, "Help Is a Four Letter Word," Goes the Weasel, March 7, 2011, http://goes-the-weasel.com/2011/03/07/help-is-a-four-letter-word/. Used with permission.

22. Mark 12:41–44.

23. This specific wording is found in Romans 12:13. Other hospitality commands include Leviticus 19:33; Isaiah 58:10–12; Luke 14:12–23; Galatians 6:9–10; 1 Timothy 3:2; 5:10; Titus 1:8; Hebrews 13:2; 1 Peter 4:9. In addition, the Bible is full of stories and examples and hospitality role models, including Jesus.

24. Luke 24:13–24.

25. Ron Hall and Denver Moore with Lynn Vincent, *Same Kind of Different as Me* (Nashville: Thomas Nelson, 2006).

chapter eight: living in the light

1. I have changed his name and some details here to protect her privacy.

2. It's important to clarify here that secrets and lies are not the same things. Secrets can *become* lies. But protecting a confidence, for example, is not necessarily the same as lying.

3. Allan Schwartz, "Family Secrets," April 25, 2007, www.mentalhelp.net/poc/view_doc.php?type=doc&id=12526&cn=51).

4. Genesis 3:6–23.

5. "The Holy Eucharist, Rite One," *The Book of Common Prayer* (New York: Church Hymnal Corporation), 323.

6. Genesis 4:1.

7. I tell that story in my book *Confessions of a Good Christian Girl* (Nashville: Thomas Nelson, 2007).

8. 1 John 1:5–9.

9. 1 John 1:5. See John 14:6; Psalm 51:6; Psalm 38:9; Job 28:11.

10. Ecclesiastes 3:7.

11. Stories from the Old Testament include Jacob (Gen. 27), Moses (Ex. 2:1–10), Tamar (Gen. 38), and David (1 Sam. 23:13–29). Jesus' secrets are mentioned in Matthew 8:4, 16:20; Mark 7:36, 8:30, 9:9; and Luke 5:14, 8:56. His instructions about praying in secret are found in Matthew 6:6. References to the early church hiding because of persecution can be found in many historical references.

12. David P. Gushee, "The Truth about Deceit," *Christianity Today,* March 1, 2006, www.christianitytoday.com/ct/2006/march/23.68.html.

13. Ephesians 4:15.